GRATITUDE WORKS!

A Twenty-One-Day Program for Creating Emotional Prosperity

ROBERT A. EMMONS

JOSSEY-BASS
A Wiley Imprint
www.josseybass.com

Cover image: ©aleksandarvelasevic/istock

Cover design: JPuda

Published by Jossey-Bass
A Wiley Imprint
One Montgomery Street, Suite 1200, San Francisco, CA 94104–4594—www.josseybass.com

Jossey-Bass books and products are available through most bookstores. To contact Jossey-Bass directly
call our Customer Care Department within the U.S. at 800-956-7739, outside the U.S. at
317-572-3986, or fax 317-572-4002.

Wiley also publishes its books in a variety of electronic formats and by print-on-demand. Some
material included with standard print versions of this book may not be included in e-books or in
print-on-demand. If the version of this book that you purchased references media such as CD or DVD
that was not included in your purchase, you may download this material at http://booksupport.wiley
.com. For more information about Wiley products, visit www.wiley.com.

All scripture quotations, unless otherwise indicated, are taken from the Holy Bible, New International
Version®, NIV®. Copyright ©1973, 1978, 1984, 2011 by Biblica, Inc.™ Used by permission of
Zondervan. All rights reserved worldwide. www.zondervan.com The "NIV" and "New International
Version" are trademarks registered in the United States Patent and Trademark Office by Biblica, Inc.™

Library of Congress Cataloging-in-Publication Data
Emmons, Robert A.
    Gratitude works! : a twenty-one-day program for creating emotional prosperity / Robert A.
Emmons. — First edition.
        pages   cm
    Includes bibliographical references and index.
    ISBN 978-1-118-13129-9 (cloth); ISBN 978-1-118-41905-2 (ebk);
    ISBN 978-1-118-42085-0 (ebk); ISBN 978-1-118-43372-0 (ebk)
    1. Gratitude   2. Gratitude—Religious aspects—Christianity.   3. Happiness.   I. Title.
BF575.G68E458   2013
179'.9—dc23

                                                                                    2012048780

Printed in the United States of America
FIRST EDITION
HB Printing   10 9 8 7 6 5 4 3 2

Contents

* * *

Preface

Consider these recent headlines: "Want to Be Happier? Be More Grateful," "The Formula for Happiness: Gratitude Plays a Part," "Teaching Gratitude, Bringing Happiness to Children," and my personal favorite, "Key to Happiness Is Gratitude, and Men May be Locked Out."

Buoyed by research findings from the field of positive psychology, the happiness industry is alive and flourishing in the United States. Each of these headlines includes the explicit assumption that gratitude should be part of any twelve-step, thirty-day, or ten-key program to develop happiness. In modern times gratitude has become untethered from its moral moorings, and collectively we are worse off because of this. When the ancient Roman philosopher Cicero stated that gratitude was the queen of the virtues, he most assuredly did not mean that gratitude was merely a stepping stone toward personal happiness. Gratitude is a morally complex disposition, and reducing this virtue to a technique or strategy to improve one's mood is to do it an injustice.

Even restricting gratitude to an inner feeling is insufficient. In the history of ideas, gratitude is considered an action (returning a favor) that is not only virtuous in and of itself but also valuable to society. To reciprocate is the right thing to do. In a book whose title translates "On Duties," Cicero wrote, "There is no duty more indispensable that that of returning a kindness."[1] Cicero's contemporary, Seneca, maintained that "he who receives a benefit with gratitude repays the first installment on his debt."[2] Neither believed that the feeling involved in returning a favor was particularly crucial. Conversely, across time, ingratitude has been treated as a serious vice, a greater vice than gratitude is a virtue. Ingratitude is the "essence of vileness," wrote the great German philosopher Immanuel Kant, and David Hume opined that ingratitude is "the most horrible and unnatural crime that a person is capable of committing."[3]

Don't get me wrong. Gratitude *does* matter for happiness. As someone who for the past decade has contributed to the scientific literature on gratitude and well-being, I would certainly grant that. The tools and techniques of modern science have been used to increase understanding of the nature of gratitude and why it is important for human flourishing more generally. From childhood to old age, accumulating evidence documents the wide array of psychological, physical, and relational benefits associated with gratitude. Yet I have come to the realization that by taking a "gratitude lite" approach we have cheapened gratitude. Gratitude lite does not do justice to its complexities. Gratitude is important not only because it helps us *feel good* but also because it inspires us to *do good*. Gratitude heals, energizes, and transforms lives in myriad ways consistent with the notion that virtue is its own reward and produces other rewards.

To give a flavor of these research findings, dispositional gratitude has been found to be positively associated with qualities such as empathy, forgiveness, and the willingness to help others. For example, people who rate themselves as having a grateful disposition perceive themselves as having more socially helpful characteristics, expressed by their empathetic behavior and emotional support for friends within the last month. In our research, when people report feeling grateful, thankful, and appreciative in their daily lives, they also feel more loving, forgiving, joyful, and enthusiastic. Notably, the family, friends, partners, and others who surround them consistently report that people who practice gratitude are viewed as more helpful, more outgoing, more optimistic, and more trustworthy.

Cicero, Seneca, Kant, and the other philosophers knew long ago what modern social science is now demonstrating. Gratitude takes us outside our scope so we see ourselves as part of a larger, intricate network of sustaining relationships, relationships that are mutually reciprocal. In this sense, similar to other social emotions, it functions to help regulate relationships, solidifying and strengthening them. Herein lies the energizing and motivating quality of gratitude. It is a positive state of mind that gives rise to the passing on of the gift through positive action. As such, gratitude serves as a key link in the dynamic between receiving and giving. It is not only a response to kindnesses received but it also motivates the recipient's future benevolent actions.

Through the ages, the virtue of gratitude has played a central role in debates over human nature. Yet outside of happiness, gratitude's benefits are rarely discussed these days; indeed, in contemporary US society, we've come to overlook, dismiss, or even disparage the significance of gratitude as a virtue. Expressions of gratitude to God by athletes and other public figures are met with cynicism. How can modern social science research on gratitude inform decisions on the perennial ethical questions of how one should act and what type of person should one be? Is gratitude vital to living the good life? How encouraging would it be to see headlines such as "Gratitude Powers a Sense of Purpose," "More Grateful Teens Less Likely to Be Depressed, Delinquent," "Gratitude Leads to Generous Giving," and "Gratitude Works! How Gratitude Prompts Corporate Social Responsibility"? I am encouraged to report that research along these lines is under way but much more is needed. Only then will modern research catch up with the timeless insights of the ancient moralists.

* LOOKING AHEAD *

Because it is a virtue, gratitude, at least initially, requires mental discipline. Virtues do not come easily, and in some sense, we need them as they act as a counterpart to our natural tendencies.

This is the paradox of gratitude: although the evidence is clear that cultivating gratitude in our life and in our attitude to life allows us to flourish, it can be difficult to accomplish. Developing and sustaining a grateful outlook on life is easier said than done because the choice for gratitude rarely comes without some real effort. We can put the science of gratitude to work for us, however. A number of evidence-based strategies, including self-guided journaling, reflective thinking, letter writing, and gratitude visits, have shown to be effective in creating sustainable gratefulness. We will explore all of these practices in the chapters that follow. They will help you become good at gratitude. You will find that each time you make the choice for gratitude, the next choice will be a little easier, a little more automatic, a little freer. In doing so, we open ourselves up to the limitless possibilities for a fullness that life has to offer us.

At the core of these practices is memory. Gratitude is about remembering. If there is a crisis of gratitude in contemporary life, as some have claimed, it is because we are collectively forgetful. We have lost a strong sense of gratitude about the freedoms we enjoy, a lack of gratitude toward those who lost their lives in the fight for freedom, and a lack of gratitude for all the material advantages we have. Furthermore, we don't even realize that we have become forgetful because we can't ever remember being different. The machinery in our minds that causes us to forget our benefits operates so seamlessly that we cannot detect its workings. However, grateful people draw on positive memories of being the recipients of benevolence, a giftedness that is neither earned nor deserved. This is why religious traditions are able to so effectively cultivate gratitude—litanies of remembrance encourage gratitude and religions do litanies very well. The scriptures, sayings, and sacraments-of-faith traditions inculcate gratefulness by drawing believers into a remembered relationship with a Supreme Being and with members of their faith community. A French proverb states that gratitude is the memory of the heart. The memory of the heart includes the memory of those we are dependent on just as the forgetfulness of dependence is unwillingness or inability to remember the benefits provided by others. Do you want to be a grateful person? Then remember to remember. This book will show you how.

Acknowledgments

If I am to be faithful to the teachings in these pages then the acknowledgments section would have to be as long as the remainder of this book. The list of names who have contributed in one way or another to the ideas I present is very long. I am tempted to fall back on Maureen Stapleton's Academy Award–winning speech ("I want to thank everybody I ever met in my entire life") and be done with it.

But that would be the cowardly way out. I have had the privilege of working with a number of researchers in the field of gratitude studies and have benefitted from the contributions that all of them have made. They deserve to be acknowledged. Many have become good friends. These include Phil Watkins, Alex Wood, Jeffrey Froh, Mike McCullough, Sonja Lyubomirsky, and Charlie Shelton.

I remain gratefully indebted to my agent, Esmond Harmsworth, of the Zachary Shuster Harmsworth literary agency. Esmond has been wonderfully supportive in transforming my writing from dry journal prose into material suitable for a general audience. My editor at Jossey-Bass, Sheryl Fullerton, was everything I could have asked for in an editor. This book exists because of her vision and skill in assisting me in moving from a collection of partially organized ideas to a coherent finished product. I thank her for helping me present my ideas with greater clarity and conviction.

I gratefully acknowledge the generous support of the John Templeton Foundation, especially to Kimon Sargeant, vice president of human sciences at the foundation. Stephen Post and the Institute of Unlimited Love also generously supported some of the research reported in this book. Quite apart from research funding, I have deeply valued my relationship with both of these men over the past decade.

A special thank you goes to Clara Morabito. You will read about this special woman in chapter 1. She has been an inspiration and I have cherished getting to know her over the past couple of years. Thank you, Clara, for spreading the word about the healing power of gratitude. Clara also read and commented on earlier drafts of the chapters. I am appreciative for her input.

My personal role model for gratitude has been my friend Doug Reid. I don't know how to acknowledge his influence except to say that he is the most grateful person that I know. Doug's gratitude is palpable, infectious, and imperishable. I am indebted to him for the title *Gratitude Works!* and for allowing me to use it. He inspires me to become a more grateful person.

I have learned much about gratitude from my wife, Yvonne, and our two sons, Adam and Garrett. If I have failed to express ample gratitude to them, it is not because they have not provided me with enough reasons to do so. I dedicate this book to them.

The Challenge of Gratitude

From time to time I receive correspondence from individuals who have become aware of my research on the benefits of gratitude and have become inspired to live more grateful lives. None has affected me quite so much as an e-mail I received in late January 2011 from Clara Morabito of Oldsmar, Florida (a suburb of Tampa). She contacted me to tell me about two events that might seem slight but that had massively changed her life. One of the events was a poem entitled *I Choose* that she composed shortly before her birthday a few years before:

> *I choose to be happy*
> *I choose to be grateful*
> *I choose to be caring*
> *And always be thoughtful.*

* * *

> *I choose to be well,*
> *I choose to be fine*

I choose to be healthy
All of the time.

* * *

I choose to be patient
I choose to be strong
I choose to be calm
All the day long.[1]

These are simple words but their power has been extraordinary in Clara's life. She meditates twice a day, before breakfast and before supper, always ending with her poem. Right before going to sleep, she reviews how wonderful the day has been and is thankful for it. She has had her share of health challenges but credits her vigor and positive outlook on life to her daily recitations of these words of affirmation. She has told me that reciting the poem leaves her with feelings of strength, wellness, and calmness and has kept her from having any significant illnesses since she wrote it. Although she cannot take two steps without the use of her walker, her energy is boundless. Her doctor was so impressed that he posted a framed copy of the poem in his examining room and gives out copies to his patients. She ends each e-mail with her signature closing: "In gratitude, joy, and with love, Clara."

But why did she write to me specifically? The second event that transformed her life was reading my book *Thanks!* She learned of it from her minister, Reverend Abhi Janamanchi, who, in preparation for Thanksgiving, was leading his Unitarian

Universalist congregation in Clearwater in a study of gratitude as a spiritual practice. A lifelong learner who began college in her forties, earning her magna cum laude BA degree at age fifty-six, Clara was impressed by the body of research I cited documenting the mental and physical health benefits of practicing gratitude.

She had experienced three prolonged emotional downturns: one in her late fifties, another in her mid-seventies, and the last in her mid-eighties. Each incident was triggered by a physical illness and lasted about three months. After she read my book, she understood why gratitude worked. What particularly resonated with her was my contention that gratitude is a choice. Not only that, it may have been one of the most important choices she ever made. She is convinced that the practice of gratitude, in combination with medication, has transformed her life. Clara reports that she feels truly happy and grateful every single day, and has the "compulsion" to spread the word about the power of gratitude to everyone she meets in various activities.

At ninety-two years young, she is a living testimony to the power of gratitude. She has been highly sought after as a speaker in her local community and has given lectures with titles such as "Prolongation of Life via Gratitude." Her goal is to become a centenarian and she is strongly convinced that gratitude will help her achieve that milestone.

As Clara reveals, gratitude is one of life's most vital ingredients, and there is a great deal of research that supports her experience. Clinical trials indicate that the practice of gratitude can have dramatic and lasting effects in a person's life. It can lower blood pressure, improve immune function, promote happiness and well-being, and spur acts of helpfulness, generosity, and cooperation.[2] Whether it springs from the glad acceptance of another's kindness, an appreciation for the majesty of nature, a recognition of the gifts in one's own life, or from countless other enchanted moments, gratitude enhances nearly all spheres of human experience. Beyond its ability to create tangible benefits, people cherish simply feeling grateful for its own sake. Some of the best moments in life are those in which we sense we have been the beneficiary of goodness freely and generously bestowed on us.

Throughout the ages, in every culture and in numerous different ways, we have been exhorted repeatedly with the same fundamental message: to live in appreciation of life's gifts, to be grateful to those who are good to us, to not take things for granted, and to avoid, at all costs, accusations of ingratitude. Yet genuinely grateful emotions and related attitudes are not as prevalent as we might assume. When was the last time you wrote a letter of heartfelt thanks to someone who had gone out of his or her way to assist you? Most of us recognize the ways in which our lives are supported and sustained by others—close or distant, living or deceased, familiar or unknown to us. But acknowledging this awareness takes effort. We more naturally think of ourselves before we think of others so it should come as no shock that grateful attitudes, along with their numerous benefits, are fleeting for most of us. Feeling grateful too often depends on our self-absorbed view of external events rather than being a basic orientation toward life. Opening ourselves to the majestic moments in our lives naturally redirects our attention to the gifts that surround us.

Most of us find it relatively easy to feel happily grateful when life proceeds according to plan — however, that is rarely the norm. It is too easy to shunt aside, overlook, or take for granted the basic gifts of life. At the other end of the spectrum, a tragedy or crisis can often elicit feelings of grateful relief that the situation did not turn out worse than it might have or incite feelings of gratitude for escaping a potentially life-threatening event. But once the crisis has passed, research has shown that we often fall back into old patterns of self-centered, unappreciative thought and action.

Although most of us intuitively know that we should feel grateful when others do us a good turn and may even realize that we function best when experiencing grateful emotions, why don't we seek such responses more consistently in our day-to-day lives? Why does genuine gratitude remain a transient and unpredictable occurrence for most people? Is it a built-in limitation? Our minds do have a built-in tendency to perceive an input as negative. In other words, our reactions to situations, to people around us, to the events of the day, what we notice and pay attention to more often than not will drift to what is going wrong rather than what is going right. To use an analogy from neuroscientist Rick Hanson, our minds are Velcro for negative information but Teflon for positive.[3] When it comes to sustaining a grateful outlook, this built-in bias does not help. It leads us to either ignore or take for granted the blessings of life although we have no problem harping on what irritates us.

I suspect that the problem is fundamentally about motivation and entrenched thought patterns rather than biology. My scientific study of gratitude since about 2000 has led me to conclude that a key factor is a fundamental lack of skill in managing our mental and emotional states and feelings.[4] In other words, we generally do not try to actively infuse our daily experiences with gratefulness because we sincerely do not know how. We all have the tools to transform virtually every moment into gratitude. Sometimes we misplace these tools and sometimes we let them become dull from disuse. If you can rediscover and learn to sharpen your gratitude tools, you will realize that nearly every waking moment provides an opportunity to practice gratitude. Gratitude clearly matters but how can we get more of it? Science has begun to illuminate the best practices for creating sustained gratitude but this information has yet to be communicated to a wide audience. That is my goal in writing this book.

There is frequently a divide between what we know we ought to do and how we actually wind up behaving. Psychologists call this the *knowledge to performance gap*. Similarly, there is a gulf between knowing that we *ought* to feel grateful and how we usually *do* feel. The depressing reality is that people often fail to live up to what they know they should do or even want to do. The Apostle Paul confessed long ago,

> I do not understand what I do. For what I want to do I do not do, but what I hate I do. And if I do what I do not want to do, I agree that the law is good. As it is, it is no longer I myself who does it, but it is sin living in me. I know that nothing good lives in me, that is, in my sinful nature. For I have the desire to do what is good, but I cannot carry it out.

For what I do is not the good I want to do; no, the evil I do not want to do—this I keep on doing. (Romans 7:15–19)

At some point in their lives, virtually all people fail to live up to their ideals. I may profess gratitude and then find myself filled with a spirit of entitlement. Instead of counting blessings, I keep (even unconsciously) a mental list of the ways in which life continually disappoints. I might encourage my children to write a thank-you note, then fail to do the same myself. I can give lectures and write articles on gratitude, then forget to thank my audiences or my editor. For gratitude to work, we must identify the barriers to gratitude and develop practical strategies to overcome them. Progress in growing the attitudes and practices of gratitude is anything but guaranteed.

This is a book of practices. It is all about the concrete things you can do to grow your mind and direct your actions toward gratefulness. I have found the organic metaphor of *growing gratitude* to be a powerful way of conveying basic truths about the nature of this quality. It is about *cultivating* a grateful disposition, which is an inclination that can become deeply ingrained. Through practice, giving thanks *grows* from the *ground* of one's being. Grateful feelings, once *buried*, can *surface* if we take the time to notice and reflect. A Russian proverb says that "gratitude waters old friendships and makes new ones sprout."[5] Gratitude is like fertilizer for the mind, spreading connections and improving its function in nearly every realm of experience. This book provides you many tools for growing your gratitude.

In *Thanks!* I wrote that legendary investor and philanthropist Sir John Templeton had posed the question, "How can we get six billion people around the world to practice gratitude?"[6] Not long after Sir John died in 2008, his daughter-in-law Pina Templeton discovered a curious document in his personal archives. It was a short letter the visionary had included with his family Christmas card mailed out in 1962. Instead of using the letter in the way it is nowadays to showcase his children's accomplishments or the family's annual vacation, he took the occasion to encourage readers to think of the mind as a garden and themselves as responsible for tending it:

> If you exercise no control, it will become a weed patch and a source of shame and misery. If you exercise wise control, then it will be filled with God's miracles and become a place of indescribable beauty. You are free to choose which. How can you do it? Simply, for example, develop a habit of looking at each thought as you would a plant. If it is worthy, if it fits the plan you desire for your mind, cultivate it. If not, replace it. How do you get it out of your mind? Simply by putting in its place two or three thoughts of love or worship, for no mind can dwell on more than two or three thoughts at one time.
>
> Circumstances outside the garden of your mind do not shape you. You shape them. For example, if you expect treachery, allowing those thoughts to dwell in your mind, you will get it. If you fill your mind with thoughts of love, you will give love and get it. If you think little of God, He will be far from you. If you think often of God, the Holy Spirit will

dwell more in you. The glory of the universe is open to every man. Some look and see. Some look and see not.

Gardens are not made in a day. God gave you one lifetime for the job. Control of your garden or your mind grows with practice and study of the wisdom other minds have bequeathed to you. He who produces an item of unique beauty in his garden or his mind may have a duty to give that seed to others. As your body is the dwelling place of your mind, so is your mind the dwelling place of your soul. The mind you develop is your dwelling place for all your days on earth, and the soul you develop on earth may be the soul you are stuck with for eternity. God has given you the choice.[7]

My hope is that this book will give you all of the gardening tools that you need to shape and grow your grateful thoughts and to weed-whack the ungrateful ones.

* PRACTICES FOR CULTIVATING GRATITUDE *

As showcased in my previous book *Thanks!*, groundbreaking research has shown that when people regularly cultivate gratitude, they experience a multitude of psychological, physical, interpersonal, and spiritual benefits. Gratitude has one of the strongest links to mental health and satisfaction with life of any personality trait—more so than even optimism, hope, or compassion. Grateful people experience higher levels of positive emotions such as joy, enthusiasm, love, happiness, and optimism, and gratitude as a discipline protects us from the destructive impulses of envy, resentment, greed, and bitterness. People who experience gratitude can cope more effectively with everyday stress, show increased resilience in the face of trauma-induced stress, recover more quickly from illness, and enjoy more robust physical health. Many of these effects are quantifiable. Consider these eye-popping statistics. People are 25 percent happier if they keep gratitude journals, sleep one-half hour more per evening, and exercise 33 percent more each week compared to persons who are not keeping these journals. Hypertensives can achieve up to a 10 percent reduction in systolic blood pressure and decrease their dietary fat intake by up to 20 percent.[8] Experiencing gratitude leads to increased feelings of connectedness, improved relationships, and even altruism. We have also found that when people experience gratitude, they feel more loving, more forgiving, and closer to God. Dozens of research studies with diverse participant groups have also revealed that the practice of gratitude leads to the following:

- Increased feelings of energy, alertness, enthusiasm, and vigor
- Success in achieving personal goals
- Better coping with stress
- A sense of closure in traumatic memories
- Bolstered feelings of self-worth and self-confidence
- Solidified and secure social relationships
- Generosity and helpfulness
- Prolonging of the enjoyment produced by pleasurable experiences
- Improved cardiac health through increases in vagal tone
- Greater sense of purpose and resilience

The evidence on practicing gratitude contradicts the widely held view that all people have a set point of, or predisposition to, happiness that cannot be reset. The luck of the genetic draw has some of us happier and some of us less happy from the start. However, the science of happiness has taught us that we can do a great deal about our sense of happiness, regardless of our set point. In some cases, people have reported that gratitude led to transformative life changes, as was true with Clara, whose story opened this chapter. All in all, science confirms that the life-giving practice of gratitude broadens our lives by enabling healing of the past, providing contentment in the present, and delivering hope for the future.

I pioneered the use of gratitude journaling as a research methodology in which people counted their blessings by systematically putting their thoughts and feelings down on paper. This powerful exercise encourages reflection that allows us to regain perspective and a sense of control over the events that move through our lives. Several hundred persons between the ages of eight and eighty have now practiced gratitude journaling under controlled experimental conditions and we have scientific evidence of what works and what doesn't. I will be applying the insights of this research throughout this book.

It might be argued that techniques such as gratitude journaling are so commonplace (and perhaps so patently obvious) that they require no further explanation. Some even think that counting blessings is a corny or cheesy activity. I would beg to differ, based on a number of nonobvious and even counterintuitive findings that have recently been reported in the gratitude literature.[9] Consider the following:

- Occasional gratitude journaling (e.g., twice weekly) boosts well-being more than the regular practice (e.g., every day) of counting blessings. Sometimes less is more. You avoid gratitude fatigue this way.
- Remembering one's sorrows, failures, and other painful experiences is more beneficial to feeling grateful than is recalling only successes. A reversal of fortune—a redemptive twist in your life when a difficult challenge was conquered—primes the pump of gratitude. Recall a breakthrough you had in what was once an insurmountable problem and be grateful for that breakthrough.
- As an illustration of the previous point, thinking about one's own death (not usually viewed as a pleasant experience) increases gratitude. Imagining a near-death experience increases people's levels of gratitude and at the same time decreases their overall level of unhappiness.
- Becoming aware that a very pleasant experience is about to end enhances feelings of gratefulness associated with it. For example, instead of worrying about all that work that will be waiting for you when you return to the office, really savor the last few days of your vacation.
- Thinking about the absence of something positive in your life produces more gratitude and happiness than imagining its presence. What would your life be like if you had not met your spouse? If you did not live in your current neighborhood? If

you had not had that chance encounter with the stranger on the plane who later became a business associate?

• Watching a dreary, depressing film will make you feel more joy and gratitude in your life than will watching a comedy.

Gratitude works but not always in the manner that we think it does or for the reasons that we think it does. I would not have necessarily predicted any of these findings, all of which have been verified by controlled experiments. By including surprising research findings such as these, I hope this book will stretch your assumptions about the nature of gratitude and how best to cultivate it. You will get the most out of this book if you try out these ideas yourself. In the final chapter I provide a series of exercises that guide you through a twenty-one-day gratitude challenge. I have organized the practices around a twenty-one-day period because the daily gratitude journaling studies demonstrated that three weeks was sufficient to lead to significant personal changes. At the end of these twenty-one days you will find yourself energized, inspired, and motivated further to make these practices a regular part of your life. People around you will notice that you have changed for the better. You will be better. And you will have accomplished it all yourself.

* DEVELOPING A GRATEFUL DISPOSITION *

Twenty-one days may not be long enough to enact a change in your fundamental outlook on life but it can set you on the path toward growing in gratefulness. There is a difference between fleeting experiences of gratitude and sustainable levels of the trait. There are layers and levels to gratitude. To have a momentary experience of gratitude is not the same as having a well-honed grateful disposition. People who are disposed toward gratitude are more apt to notice what is going right in their lives, seeing the role that others play in these good things, and expressing gratitude toward others in words or in deeds. They are prone to not taking things for granted. They have developed the skills of noticing, appreciating, and communicating. Individuals with the disposition toward gratitude would strongly endorse such statements as the following:

- It's important to appreciate each day that you are alive.
- I often reflect on how much easier my life is because of the efforts of others.
- For me, life is much more of a gift than it is a burden.
- One of my favorite times of the year is Thanksgiving.
- I'm basically very thankful for the parenting that was provided to me.
- I could not have gotten where I am today without the help of many people.
- It seems that I can even find reasons to feel thankful for bad things that happen.
- I have been so struck by the beauty or awe of something that I felt grateful in return.
- If I had to list everything that I felt grateful for, it would be a very long list.
- I find it easy to express gratitude to those who have helped me.

You will be able to take a questionnaire to measure your own level of gratefulness in chapter 7.

To illustrate differences between more grateful and less grateful persons, compare a hypothetical child "Bo," who always seems to have a deeply grateful heart no matter what the circumstance, to "Nathaniel," who at his best can barely grunt "thanks" after he has been done a favor. I believe most people would agree that Bo and Nathaniel illustrate, qualitatively speaking, distinct gradients of gratitude. At their respective birthday parties, Bo unwraps each present slowly, savoring the experience and his expressions and words reveal joyful appreciation toward the giver. Nathaniel, by contrast, rushes through his pile of presents, tearing off the paper at breakneck speed, and after he has opened the last looks around to see if there are more. Even relatively early in life, the differences in how they respond to situations that call for gratitude are apparent. It would not be fair to say that Nathaniel is an ungrateful lost cause but it is clear that they have two very distinct approaches to life based on how they respond to what they have been given. Because life is mostly about giving, receiving, and repaying based on the reactions to what we receive in life, this fundamental orientation is likely to lead to very different downstream consequences for Bo and Nathaniel. Which one will be happier? More alive and vibrant? Better liked? More effective in life? Who will have more obstacles to being fulfilled? In chapter 6 I explore some of the basic obstacles to gratitude and how these might be overcome.

Bo and Nathaniel would also differ in various components of the grateful disposition. My colleagues and I identified four different facets of gratitude, each representing a different dimension along which to characterize a grateful person. The first facet of the grateful disposition might be called gratitude *intensity*. A person with a strong grateful disposition who experienced a positive event would be expected to feel more intensely grateful than would someone less disposed toward gratitude who experienced the same positive event. A second facet of the grateful disposition might be called gratitude *frequency*. Someone with a strong grateful disposition might report feeling grateful several times per day, and gratitude might be elicited by even the simplest favor or act of politeness. Conversely, for someone less disposed toward gratitude, such a favor or act of politeness might be insufficient to elicit gratitude. As a result, the person with a weaker grateful disposition might experience less gratitude within a specified time period (e.g., hours, days, or weeks).

A third facet of the grateful disposition might be called gratitude *span*, which refers to the number of life circumstances for which a person feels grateful at a given time. People with a strong grateful disposition might feel grateful for their families, their jobs, their health, and life itself, along with a wide variety of other benefits. People less disposed toward gratitude might be aware of experiencing gratitude for fewer aspects of their lives. A fourth facet of the grateful disposition might be called gratitude *density*, which refers to the number of persons to whom one feels grateful for a single positive outcome or life circumstance. When asked to whom one feels grateful for a certain outcome, say, obtaining a good job, someone with a strong grateful disposition density might list a large number of others, including parents, elementary school teachers, tutors, mentors, fellow students, and God. Someone less disposed toward gratitude might feel grateful to fewer people.

As you monitor your growth in gratitude, I encourage you to think in terms of these four facets of the grateful disposition. Try to figure out where your weaknesses lie and where your strengths lie. Maybe it is relatively easy for you to feel intense gratitude at times (intensity, a plus), but you do not feel it very often (lack of frequency, which is a negative). Or perhaps you have a very small gratitude span. A student in one of my classes journaled that she was grateful for only three things in her life: her Maine coon cat, her rat terrier, and her apartment where the three of them harmoniously dwelled. If you are like her, try to expand your span by elaborating on your truncated list. Work actively at finding more to be grateful for. When you grow in gratitude, you grow all over.

Surely a deep and abiding gratefulness, the ability to relish the little pleasures that common occurrences afford, is a desirable human quality. Yet insomuch as gratitude typically is a *response* to a gift, how can one actually cultivate it as a disposition? Doesn't gratitude require another person or being to provide a benefit to the receiver? In that view, I am at the mercy of others to provide or withhold favors. When seen this way, gratefulness can be seen as more like courage because one has to wait until appropriate opportunities arise in which to act courageously or conversely, cowardly. It would not make sense to cultivate a trait of courageousness in any generalized sense.

But can gratefulness be seen differently? Does it have to depend on others or can we cultivate it as a way of being? Among the questions I will explore in this book are the following:

- How do we get from *feeling* gratitude to *being* grateful?
- Is gratitude one of those "unfair" gifts given to those who possess sunny dispositions, those who do not instinctively feel the anxiety, pain, and separation of living in this world?
- Can we choose to cultivate the trait of gratitude?
- Is there a way to lower our threshold to perceive kindnesses or to imbue everyday experiences within an emotional backdrop of gratefulness?
- What are the mental tools that allow this?

A recent study does suggest that there is an influence of genes on levels of gratitude. Researchers at the University of Minnesota estimated the heritability of gratitude at about 40 percent.[10] This indicates that although gratitude may be influenced by genetic factors, the majority of a given person's disposition toward gratitude is determined by nongenetic influences over which a person has more personal control. So it is not the case that you either have gratitude or you don't. The genetic programming here is not strong. We can all have it and we can have more of it if we systematically train ourselves to pay attention to what is going right in our lives, to see the contributions that others make in these good things, and express gratitude verbally and behaviorally. It's my hope that the practices and guidelines offered in this book will have the same impact in your life that it had in Clara Morabito's life. I urge you to take up the gratitude challenge that this book offers.

Journaling for Gratitude

There are no positive psychology Olympic games, but if there were and gratitude journaling was a sport, Jane Randall of Centerville, Utah, would likely be the world record holder. When she contacted me a few years ago, she told me that she had been keeping a gratitude journal for more than eighteen years and that she had listed 18,256 blessings "so far." Remarkably, she told me that she tried to list each blessing only once, which forced her to be very specific and to search for and appreciate even trite blessings, such as "being grateful I didn't grind up any spoons in the garbage disposal today." As impressive as her journaling is, her record, though, may be in jeopardy because I recently heard from a woman from West Virginia who claimed a list exceeding over twenty-three thousand entries. You might not be currently at the level of these supercharged gratitude journalers but developing an increased awareness of and appreciation for the small blessings of life can be done with patient and sustained practice.

Neither of these individuals had particularly easy lives. Nor did writing come easily or naturally for them. Jane confided that she had suffered from gratitude fatigue hundreds of times and would have sometimes preferred to be writing a journal of grudges. She'd lost the urge to journal on several occasions, most notably when her brother-in-law took his own life, but she always came back. My West Virginian journaler grew up with alcoholic father and emotionally distant mother. For years she filled notebooks with depressed thoughts, was hospitalized for depression several times, even received electroconvulsive therapy twice. Then she discovered gratitude journaling and rid herself of her "382,483,112 books on depression that I don't need and never helped me."

Their stories are poignant but not atypical. Over the years I have been contacted by people from all walks of life similar to these. They have included survivors of child abuse, prison inmates, persons with terminal cancer and other health afflictions, CEOs of large organizations, doctors and lawyers, truck drivers, moms, dads, teachers, pastors, students, athletes, Democrats, Republicans, and atheists. Whether or not they actively journal, what unites them is their strong conviction that gratitude works!

One of the most inspiring communications that I have received was from DeMarcus Betts, incarcerated at the Bellamy Creek Correctional Facility in Ionia, Michigan. Mr. Betts had read an interview with me printed in *USA*

Today. Shortly after the article appeared, I receive a two-page hand-scrawled letter from him:

> I humbly apologize Sir for intruding upon your "psyche" but as so affected I am by your short, yet treasurable words in USA Today, Nov. 18, 2010 about "GRATITUDE."
>
> Since there is no such thing as a perfect letter or person, I will just be candid and direct as I usually am. Please bear with me.
>
> Expect nothing, appreciate EVERYTHING! is the 4 word motto I've lived by for the past years. I can look up to the sky and smile at the radiance of the sun. How so? Especially since my life is so gloomy, self-destructive, and unpredictable most days??? Well, it's because of the fact that IT COULD ALWAYS BE WORSER! I could write 5 books about my life journey that's how eventful it has been, mostly negative though. But one thing that constantly amazes me about life is that universal adversities all leave mental scar tissue. Mind you sir, I am far from an intelligent man (in any scholarly sense anyway) I don't even possess a G.E.D. (yet) and I'm 35 years old. But I do comprehend the beauty in being THANKFUL for my every breath. And it doesn't revolve around any religious concepts or doctrines either. As a matter of honesty, I'm not one of the many prisoners who "profess religion" since incarceration has fallen upon me.
>
> I just take pleasures from one experience to the next. I don't know if I'll get paroled in 7 yrs, 10, or 20 years, but whatever tomorrow brings, I'll do exactly what I am doing today. And that is APPRECIATING my every moment.

Simple and plain. People like yourself help to inspire me
even further in my convictions[1]

* THE ROAD TO GRATEFULNESS *

One of the best ways to cultivate gratitude is to establish a daily
practice in which you remind yourself of the gifts, grace, benefits, and good things you enjoy. When we are grateful, we
affirm that sources of goodness exist in our lives. By writing
each day, we magnify and expand on these sources of goodness.
Setting aside time on a daily basis to recall moments of gratitude associated with even mundane or ordinary events, personal attributes one has, or valued people one encounters has
the potential to weave together a sustainable life theme of
gratefulness just as it nourishes a fundamentally affirming life
stance. US Buddhist teacher Jack Kornfield writes the following in *The Wise Heart*:

> Gratitude is a gracious acknowledgement of all that sustains
> us, a bow to our blessings, great and small. Gratitude is the
> confidence in life itself. In it, we feel the same force that
> pushes grass through cracks in the sidewalk, invigorating
> our own life. In Tibet, the monks and nuns even offer
> prayers of gratitude for the suffering they have been given:
> "Grant that I might have enough suffering to awaken in me
> the deepest possible compassion and wisdom." Gratitude
> does not envy or compare. Gratitude receives in wonder the
> myriad offering of rain and sunlight, the care that supports
> every single life. As gratitude grows it gives rise to joy.[2]

Gratitude journaling was famously publicized by Oprah Winfrey in the late 1990s, and we now have research evidence of what works and what does not. In 1998 my colleague Mike McCullough and I designed a program of research to examine the effect of a gratitude practice on psychological and physical well-being. In our first study, we randomly assigned college student participants one of three tasks, each of which created distinct comparison conditions. They either briefly described, in a single sentence, five things they were grateful for *(the gratitude condition)*, five hassles *(the hassles condition)*, or five events or circumstances that affected them *(events condition)*. Hassles are relatively minor, everyday stressful circumstances such as not being able to find a babysitter, dealing with the rising price of gas, doing laundry, misplacing one's wallet. The time frame for each of these was the past week. Participants completed these exercises along with a variety of other measures of health and happiness once per week for ten consecutive weeks.

A wide range of experiences sparked gratitude: cherished interactions, awareness of physical health, overcoming obstacles, and simply being alive, to name a few. Some of the specific blessings listed by participants were "that my in-laws live only ten minutes away, warmth of sun on my skin, doctor removed ear wax from ear, it rained, heard we are going to be great-grandparents (again), my checkbook balanced, my freedom living in the USA, grateful for being single because of my friend's problems, and my life considering that I almost lost it because of domestic violence." Examples of hassles included "roommates are filthy animals, having to buy

Mother's Day card at the last minute, somebody snapped the antenna off my car, people who stand with their carts in middle of aisle at the store, running out of money and having to ask parents for more."

The results were quite striking and garnered considerable media attention after they were published. The study became the most cited article I have published in twenty-five years.[3] Participants in the gratitude condition felt better about their life as a whole and were more optimistic about the future than participants in either of the other control conditions. To put it into numbers, they were a full 25 percent happier than the other participants. Those in the gratitude condition reported fewer health complaints and even spent more time exercising than control participants did. They spent a whopping 30 percent more time exercising. Thus, something as simple as counting blessings once a week resulted in significant emotional and health benefits. Because of the logic of random assignment, I was convinced that the differences were caused by the gratitude task and did not reflect preexisting differences between the groups.

Intrigued by these results, we made gratitude a daily practice over a three-week period in our second study.[4] As in the first experiment, participants were randomly assigned to one of three conditions. In the second study, the gratitude and hassles conditions remained identical to those used in the first study but we changed the events condition to one in which participants were encouraged to think about ways in which they were better off than others (the social comparison condition). We wanted participants to think about advantages or privileges they possessed relative to others, believing that this would provide a more stringent comparison with the group counting their blessings. Research has shown that a downward social comparison can be effective in coping with stress. In one famous study, women with breast cancer who'd had a lumpectomy were less distressed if they'd compared themselves to younger women who'd had either a single or double mastectomy.[5]

The gratitude condition still showed an impressive array of benefits despite the fact that the social comparison condition may have mimicked it and produced some grateful feelings. Although the health benefits seen in the first study were not evident in the second study (perhaps because of the short duration of the intervention), participants in the gratitude condition felt more joyful, enthusiastic, interested, attentive, energetic, excited, determined, and stronger than those in the hassles condition. They also reported offering others more emotional support or help with a personal problem, indicating that the gratitude condition increased compassion and generosity—and more directly supported the notion that gratitude makes good things happen. Again, those in the gratitude condition showed significantly more positive feelings than those in the hassles condition. Our second study even produced evidence that the twenty-one-day practice led to greater increases in gratitude than did the weekly practice.

Strikingly, our participants continued to keep gratitude journals long after the study ended, and when we contacted them, months later, they commented on the long-term benefits of being in the study. One individual told us that "being forced, consciously to reflect, contemplate and sum up my life on a daily basis was curiously therapeutic, and enlightening. I was reminded of facets of myself that I very much like and others that could use improvement . . . I have tried to become more aware of my level of gratitude." Practicing gratitude is self-sustaining. No external incentive is needed.

Gratitude journaling promotes the savoring of positive life experiences and situations so that we can distill the maximum satisfaction and enjoyment from them. This promotes a shift in consciousness from what we are lacking to the abundance that surrounds us. Gratitude leads us to affirm and acknowledge the good things in our lives. In addition, the ability to appreciate our life circumstances may also help us cope by training us to positively reinterpret stressful or negative life experiences, bolster our coping resources, and strengthen our social relationships. And because you can't be grateful and negative at the same time, it counteracts feelings of envy, anger, greed, and other states harmful to happiness.

Of course, none of us can be commanded to be grateful, any more than we can command people to love or to forgive. What we tried to do in our research was to have participants focus their attention on benefits they have received, using the language of benefits in the broadest possible way. Turning the mind to that which has been present all along drives long-term positive outcomes in virtually every sphere of functioning that we have examined. Our thoughts, our moods, our relationships, our health, our lives—everything changes!

* EYES WIDE OPEN IN GRATITUDE *

From these systematically controlled experimental studies on journaling we learned that a daily practice of cataloging gratitude-inspiring events in your life will clearly make you happier and healthier and less negative. I am often asked if there is a key to journaling. There is no one right way to do it. It does not much matter whether you begin each day journaling or make your list the last thing you do at the end of the day. You don't need to buy an expensive personal journal, download an app to help you record your entries, or worry about spelling or grammar. The important thing is to establish the daily habit of paying attention to gratitude-inspiring events. At the end of the chapter I give you my top ten tips for effective gratitude journaling. All of these practices begin with the following: keep your eyes wide open in gratitude! David Steindl-Rast is a Benedictine monk who grew up in Nazi-occupied Austria and has concluded that in order to be fully alive, we must open our eyes in gratitude, to see the wonders of the world that surround us. We go through our days in a daze, he says. How tragic! Each day is a gift. Today is the one gift you have been given "and the only totally appropriate response is gratefulness."[6] Take these words seriously. Write about the gifts of the day in your journal. Respond with gratefulness.

The act of writing down your blessings translates your thoughts into words, and writing has been shown to have advantages over just thinking the thoughts. Writing helps to organize thoughts, facilitate integration, and helps you accept your own experiences and put them in context. In essence, it allows you to see the meaning of events going on around you and create meaning in your own life. Therapists often recommend writing about unpleasant, even traumatic events. This is good advice but you must do more than just rant about them. Gratitude journaling may help you bring a new and redemptive frame of reference to a difficult life situation. With eyes wide open in gratitude, we see the possibility of blessings instead of burdens. Angeles Arrien, author of *Living in Gratitude: A Journey That Will Change Your Life*, describes grateful seeing as "the ability to look first at what is good and working in our lives without minimizing or denying the hardships or challenges that are also present."[7] Here are some comments made by persons suffering from mild depression when asked to keep a gratitude journal:

- When I'm sinking and get caught up in my problems, it helps me rise above it.
- It keeps me in touch with reality out there rather than my constant negative interpretations. I remember that others are there and can be supportive.
- Helps me get out of the negative and remember that not all is lost.
- I am reminded that there is more to feel good about than to feel bad about.
- I stop taking the good in my life for granted and get out of my shell.
- I realize that it could be a lot worse.
- It helps me get out of myself.

- I am reminded of the things that make me feel good. It makes me want to do more positive things.
- I go from what is missing to what I do have.
- See the good in the people in my life rather than just their faults.
- Makes me feel safer. It helps me relax because I remember that I am supported.
- When I'm scared, it helps me remember that there is help.
- Helps me love my life a bit more.
- Makes me feel lucky rather than sorry for myself.
- It brings me back in the here and now, where I can always find something to be grateful for.
- It brings a smile across my face. Helps make the negativity vanish even for a brief moment.

Is gratitude journaling easy? If you are not in the habit of doing so, it may not be at first. I can tell you that in the beginning gratitude journaling may be discouraging; sometimes your list will seem barren. But as the ancient sages and contemporary research tells us, becoming aware of one's blessings actually leads to having more to be grateful about. There is an interesting pattern in gratitude journal entries for those who start out as the least-grateful people. The first few days, they struggle to fill the spaces on the form. By days six and seven, they list at least four blessings. After that, there is rarely a day where they do not write down five gratitudes. As our perceptual lens becomes sharpened we are more likely to notice blessings when before we saw curses. Margaret, a participant in our journaling study on gifts, wrote the following in her journal:

> A special gift today: as I was sorting out some papers, I ran across an inspirational clipping I had forgotten about—it tells about a man who was marooned on an island. Each day he prayed for rescue but none came. With much weary effort he built a hut to live in and to store provisions. Then one day the hut burned down. He cried out, "All is gone—God, how could you do this to me!" The next day a ship came to rescue him. He said, "How did you know I was here?" The reply was, "We saw your smoke signal." Remember the next time when your little hut is burning to the ground, it may be a signal that summons the grace of God. This clipping blessed me so much when I first read it—and now, today, it mysteriously showed up to bless me again and to remind me again of how many times I've been rescued when I thought all was lost.

As we document our gifts, we no longer take them *for* granted. We take them *as* granted, as they were intended to be. We begin to be grateful for the ability to feel gratitude. The spiral grows. The important thing is to get started wherever you are, even if the only item on your list is "nothing bad happened today." If you are currently at a "minus five" on an ungrateful-to-grateful scale of minus ten to plus ten, it may be necessary to first move to a zero point before you can begin to clearly see positive blessings and move to the plus side of the ledger.

When you identify in your daily journal those elements in your life for which you are grateful, consider them "gifts." As you reflect on or contemplate an aspect of your life for which you are grateful, make the conscious effort to associate it with the word *gift*. Be aware of your feelings and how you relish and savor this gift in your imagination. Many people start with nature. Check out the spectacular fall foliage. The azure blue sky. The fragrance of spring. The first rains of the season. The first snowfall. They are all gifts. Wow! Look at them. Notice them. Savor them. La Rochefoucauld said, "Happiness does not consist in things themselves but in the relish we have of them."[8] Take the time to be especially aware of the depth of your gratitude. In other words, don't hurry through this exercise as if it were just another item on your to-do list.

Peter Clemens, author of *The Change Blog* (www .thechangeblog.com/start-here), offers three practical reasons why gratitude journaling is recommended as a tool for personal transformation. First, a journal provides insight. Do you ever wonder who you really are? Do you have problems that occur again and again—patterns of behavior that you just can't break out of? Keeping a journal for an extended period of time lets you learn the truth about yourself: how your motivation waxes and wanes; how many projects you let fizzle out after a brief burst of excitement; what topics you return to again and again and again, much like the student who lists her cat, her dog, and her apartment day after day for three weeks in her gratitude journal. If you've been keeping a journal for a while (even if it's fallen by the wayside recently), read through some old entries. Do you spot any patterns? Does reading it inspire you to resume journaling with a renewed focus?

A second reason why journaling is effective is that intention leads to discipline and discipline produces results. Are you an aspiring blogger, author, poet, journalist, or writer of any description? If you're making serious attempts at writing, you need to be disciplined about it—no professional writer works just when they're "in the mood" or when "the muse descends." If you wait around for the mood to strike you, you will likely strike out. Developing the habit of writing regularly (ideally every day) will be a bigger factor in your success than your raw level of writing skill.

When I made the transition from academic journal writing to trade books, I consulted writers whom I admired to learn the tricks of the trade. Virtually all of them said that they never let a day go by when they did not write something. They would sit in front of their computers with a concrete, attainable goal. Two pages, two paragraphs, two good hours. They stayed the course until they had reached their goal for the day. Guess what they produced after a year? A finished book! The trick is to honor that commitment to write those two pages and don't stop until you reach that goal. It is motivating to see what you produce. Jane Randall (whose story opened this chapter) told me that she keeps hard copies of her lists of gifts that can be held, opened, read, and savored at any time. She also writes each blessing in complete sentences with enough detail so that she can reread the entries years later and again feel the full impact of what's listed, which also increases her motivation.

The third reason for keeping a journal is that it provides a legacy gift that you will leave to someone or even yourself. You could give your children the gift of your own gratitudes! Keeping a journal today means you can look back in five years, ten years, or in old age at the sources of goodness in your life.

* THREE KEYS TO GRATITUDE JOURNALING *

Recent studies of varieties of gratitude journaling practices indicate that specificity, surprise, and scarcity are three essential keys to unleashing blessings of gratitude. Fully understanding and implementing them greatly increase the positive effects of gratitude in your life.

Specificity: The Truth Is in the Details

When recalling a benefit that we have received from another, break it down into multiple components and reflect on each element. For example, you will be less grateful if you simply say that you are grateful to your mother for the sacrifices she made so that you could get an education than if you consciously and deliberately try to think about or overtly mention and remind yourself of, thereby, the thousands of hours and days and weeks and years of hard work that she invested on your behalf. The truth is in the details—Greg Krech, expert in Naikan therapy, reminds us that gratitude is looking at life accurately.[9] The goal of gratitude is to perceive life in its entirety, which engenders a greater sense of gratitude. If I say that I'm grateful to my wife in general or I am grateful that she has made me approximately 2,400 lunches over the seventeen years we've been married, which form of thanks is more meaningful? Of course, my gratitude does not begin and end with the sandwiches, but you get the idea. Generalizations get us farther from the truth and platitudes are not likely to be seen as authentically genuine.

Being specific is effective for two reasons. First, it helps us avoid gratitude fatigue. The more discrete the elements, the less we will cease to recognize them or take any one of them for granted. Second, specificity encourages us to appreciate the giver's efforts and recognize more of the details. For example, if I simply say that I am grateful to the coffee barista at Peet's, that is less likely to make me as grateful than if I consciously and deliberately think about how he remembers my name and the particular way that I like my latte (small, flat, and low fat). When it comes to gratitude, the truth is in the details.

There is experimental evidence that validates the importance of getting specific. Researchers at the University of Southern California arranged a study in which they varied the amount of elaboration participants were asked to do in their journaling. One group wrote five sentences about something in their lives for which they were grateful whereas another group wrote one sentence about each of five things. A third group wrote about ways in which they were better off than others. Each group completed their task online for ten weeks. Those who wrote five sentences about one thing showed they were less tired, sad, and lethargic compared with the other groups. They were also more likely to feel significantly more alert, excited, elated, and happy compared with those writing about several different things or ways in which they were better off than others.[10] Depth matters.

GRATITUDE WORKS!

Surprise: The Key to Emotional Intensity

Emotion researchers Andrew Ortony and Jerry Clore, who have explored the interaction of thinking and emotions, researched the factors that affect the intensity of emotions, that is, the magnitude or strength of the feeling; for example, an emotion such anger varies in intensity from mild annoyance to full-blown rage.[11] We all know that emotions can vary as we respond to events, real or imagined, or as we relive these events in our minds.

Ortony and Clore found that surprise was one of the primary drivers of emotional intensity. Surprises can be pleasant (as when we receive an unexpected gift) or unpleasant (as when we are shocked by an accident). All other factors being equal, events that are surprising and unexpected produce stronger emotional reactions than events that we expected or anticipated. It's not hard to think of examples of pleasant and unpleasant surprises. Recall for a moment the finest gift you ever received. I'd be willing to wager that it came as a surprise to you. Growing up, I was often unable to control the urge to hunt for Christmas presents stashed in various hiding places throughout the house. Picking up, shaking, sniffing, or otherwise attempting to figure out what was in the packages did give me an idea of what they contained but it also reduced some of the joy on Christmas morning. When we feel entitled or expect good things to happen or otherwise fail to be surprised by them, we don't feel grateful. "All goods look better when they look like gifts," wrote the prolific British author G. K. Chesterton.[12] And which gifts look better? Those that look like (and in fact are) surprises. So gifts or benefits that come as surprises create more gratitude because they are unexpected. When the IRS sends a bigger refund check than we had been expecting, most of us are extraordinarily grateful (and thankful they didn't audit us!). DeMarcus Betts showcased this in his letter to me from prison with the motto he has lived with for the past ten years: "Expect nothing, appreciate everything!"

Try to write about unexpected, novel, or unanticipated events, circumstances, and experiences or about those that you are curious about. Maybe you were uncertain about the outcome or think it could have turned out differently. Identifying surprises keeps your journaling fresh. For example, after a long weekend at a baseball tournament, I arrived home expecting leftover frozen pizza. My wife unexpectedly prepared a special dinner. My gratitude was off the charts. When I wrote about it, I pointed to my gratitude of my thoughtful spouse, to not having to eat the reheated pizza, to feeling loved and cared for, to getting a home-cooked meal, to not having to shop or cook. The surprise of it all made me feel blessed beyond description.

It's a Wonderful Life

Musing about pleasant events or circumstances is often not enough. Rather, how we think about these positive events may be the critical factor in whether we feel grateful and happy. This important discovery was made by Tim Wilson and Dan Gilbert and their colleagues in another series of experiments that have come to be known as the "George Bailey effect."[13]

Virtually everyone is familiar with Frank Capra's classic 1940s film, *It's a Wonderful Life*. In the movie, an angel named Clarence (played by Henry Travers) takes a suicidal George Bailey (played by Jimmy Stewart) on a tour of George's world as it would have been if George had never been born. Rather than asking George to count his blessings, Clarence allows him to observe a world in which those blessings never came about. This exercise forces George to realize just how rare and precious the good things in his life actually are, which instantly cures his despair. Research suggests that this cinematic Christmas classic captures a useful psychological insight. Thinking about the ways in which an event might not have occurred can make that event seem more surprising. One of the hallmarks of surprising events is that they elicit feelings, which is not the case when we encounter events or situations we take for granted or that have become routine. The Dutch affective scientist Nico Frijda speculated that "constantly being aware of how fortunate one's condition is and of how it could have been otherwise, or actually was otherwise before" rekindles recollection and imagination.[14]

Look back and imagine your life if a certain decision had been reversed or if a particular event had not transpired. How might things have turned out differently? A man in his mid-sixties wonders what would have happened if, when he was eighteen, his best friend had not introduced him to the truth claims of Jesus Christ. "What jail would I have wound up in?" he said. "Not a day goes by when I am not grateful to my childhood friend," he acknowledged to me. His life took a totally different trajectory because of the decision he made nearly a half-century before.

Wilson and Gilbert tested this insight by asking people to write about why a positive event might never have happened and therefore why it was surprising or why it was certain to be part of their lives and was not at all surprising. In Wilson and Gilbert's study, one-half of the participants were asked to think about how a positive event for which they were grateful happened easily or was not surprising. The other half of the participants were instructed to think about how a positive event might never have happened or might never have been part of their lives and to describe ways in which it was surprising that this thing or event became part of their lives.[15]

Results revealed that participants who thought about the absence of the event reported more positive feelings than those who saw it as unsurprising. Only those writing about a positive event *and* thinking about how it was surprising and might have been absent from their lives benefitted emotionally. Furthermore, those participants also reported feeling more surprised that the event occurred and said they had less understanding about why it occurred than the other participants who took it for granted. Our minds think in terms of the mental comparisons we make between the ways things are and how they might have been different. When we lament opportunities lost or regrets over what might have been, these comparisons may be counterproductive to our mental well-being. But we can harness the power of this kind of thinking by reminding ourselves of how much worse life might be than it is or how we may have never received a particular blessing in our lives.

Why is thinking about the absence of something good so beneficial? It helps counter the tendency to take benefits for granted. We take them for granted because we get so used to their presence in our lives. The process by which we return to our characteristic happiness level a short time after unusually good or bad events is known as adaptation. We adapt to our fortunes. We also adapt to misfortunes but this takes longer. Initially, people react strongly to changed circumstances but over time their emotional reactions dampen and lose power. There is actually a website containing sad stories of people who won lottery windfalls (over $1 million) and who after the initial elation wore off, wound up broke, depressed, and lonely.

Scarcity: Wanting Now What We May Not Have Later

"Praise, like gold and diamonds, owes its value only to its scarcity," wrote Samuel Johnson.[16] Studies have shown that when people are told that a positive life event is about to end, they are more likely to appreciate their experience and make more of an effort to capitalize on what remains. This awareness can be a positive motivator to pay more attention to it and therefore to feel more grateful about it. A sense of "now or never" can impel us to make the most of every day.

Jaime Kurtz of James Madison University specializes in the study of nonobvious or counterintuitive routes to happiness.[17] About six weeks prior to graduation, she asked a sample of fourth-year students to write about their college experience.

Participants were told to think either that graduation was far off or that it would happen soon. The specific instructions were, "Write about why you are grateful for your friends here, especially considering how little time (or in the other case, how much time) you have left in college." Those who focused on the impending ending of college felt a greater sense of well-being and participated in more college-related activities (spending time with those friends, engaging in activities with those friends). Once again, how a person thinks about pleasant events makes a difference. The emotional benefits are more likely to accrue when a person is framing an event as being limited in time. It is a good practice to notice that a particularly good thing in your life is going to end and not assume it will go on forever. Or just imagine that it is about to end. For example, how would you approach a valued relationship if you knew that the person would soon be moving? Would you treat the time you had left with this person differently? How could you increase your gratitude for having that person in your life? This is what you should be writing about in your journal.

* WHY NEWNESS MATTERS *

When I was an undergraduate in Maine, my first research project involved sensation seeking. Sensation seekers crave novelty, excitement, and stimulation, whether in the form of travel to exotic locales, sampling never-tried ethnic dishes, or . . . , and they are easily bored. They love bright lights and hustle and bustle and like to take risks and seek thrills.

This love of novelty appears to be rooted deep in our evolutionary past. In her book *New: Understanding Our Need for Novelty and Change*, journalist Winifred Gallagher contends that we cannot resist things that are new and different and that novelty seeking has been central to our survival as a species.[18] The benefits of novelty seeking have been explored by psychiatrist Robert Cloninger of Washington University in St. Louis.[19] Cloninger has found that those who love novelty enjoy good health, satisfying friendships, and emotional stability throughout adulthood compared to those who shy away from newness. Novelty seeking allows us to respond flexibly to the world and to the new and different in particular.

Sensation seeking, I have to say, is not one of my signature traits. I spend most days turning around sentences on my computer screen, and I have taught the same courses for the past twenty-five years at my university (although I do change my lecture notes from time to time). Yet to some extent, we all need some novelty. Variety is the spice of life, as the saying goes. And that is especially true in our gratitude lists. Without an effort to inject some newness into it, gratitude journaling can quickly become stale and cease to inspire. Our lives can be drained of gratitude if we see our circumstances and surroundings as boring and tedious.

Moreover, accumulating evidence indicates that dopamine cells in our brain, which regulate reward, pleasure, and motivation, respond most strongly when the reward is unanticipated. After a reward has become routine or expected, dopamine cell firing is substantially reduced. Thus there are neurochemical reasons why novelty and surprise are essential for effective gratitude journaling.

Shortly after Michael McCullough and I published our milestone article on the benefits of gratitude journaling, a seemingly contradictory report appeared in the *Review of General Psychology*. Sonja Lyubomirsky of the University of California, Riverside, and author of the acclaimed *The How of Happiness* reported the results of a six-week intervention in which students were instructed to contemplate "the things for which they are grateful" either once a week or three times a week. The results again suggested that timing is important. Students who regularly expressed gratitude showed increases in well-being over the course of the study but only if they performed the activity just once a week. Lyubomirsky suggested that perhaps counting their blessings several times a week led people to become bored with the practice, finding it less fresh and meaningful over time.[20] Once again, this speaks to the importance of novelty and creativity in journaling. You must do what you can to avoid gratitude fatigue. The tips at the end of this chapter will help you combat gratitude fatigue.

* DOES GRATITUDE JOURNALING CHANGE THE BRAIN? *

So much to savor, so much to be grateful for. And since I'm not sure of the address to which to send my gratitude, I put it out there in everything I do.
—MICHAEL J. FOX[21]

A complete account of why journaling for gratitude is beneficial must at some level deal with the neural basis of gratitude. Is there a neural signature to gratitude? Recent research in the neurochemistry of positive emotions may explain why surprise, novelty, and scarcity are such important components of gratitude journaling and why the process of journaling itself is so rewarding.

Similar to other emotions, your experience of gratitude is rooted in your brain's chemistry and anatomy. What happens in our brains when we feel grateful to someone? Nowadays, many of us don't believe we really understand how the mind works unless we understand the underlying brain processes that are involved. Neuroscientists are the high priests within most university communities and the lay public and academics are fascinated by the latest high-resolution brain scan images. Neurochemical research is beginning to shed light on what goes on in your brain when you acknowledge and appreciate something good that has happened to you. It's important to point out, however, that neuroscience of gratitude is in its infancy and at the present time much more is not known than is known. In the interest of full disclosure, I am not a neuroscientist. I've become convinced that I am missing the part of the brain that is needed to understand the parts of the brain. Yet I have managed to learn enough to come to the realization that neurobiological processes involved in experience and expression of gratitude can lead to new and important discoveries in why gratitude works.

It appears that hormones circulating in the blood and neurotransmitters in the brain are the chemical correlates of gratitude. For instance, we know that dopamine and serotonin circulating in certain regions of the brain are related to happiness and other pleasurable feelings. A number of converging lines of evidence indicate that the neurotransmitter dopamine modulates and is required for the short-term perception and expression of gratitude. Dopamine is distributed in the brain in such a way as to affect diverse brain systems, including motivation, salience, reward, and emotion in addition to movement and executive function. This chemical regulates reward, pleasure, and motivation—all of which are central to gratitude. Dopaminergic activity in the frontal lobes very likely influences levels of gratitude or at least the capacity to feel grateful. Dopamine juices the joy we experience when we celebrate goodness from reflecting on what is in our gratitude journals. This neurotransmitter increases the probability that a person will feel gratitude by noticing gratitude-inspiring events.[22] Moreover, accumulating evidence indicates that dopamine cells in regions of the brain sensitive to reward (the striatum and nucleus accumbens) respond most strongly to unanticipated reward. After a reward has become routine or expected, dopamine cell firing is substantially reduced. Thus we have the neurochemical reasons why novelty and surprise are essential for effective gratitude journaling.[23]

The feeling of gratitude depends on many factors, most of which are cognitive (recognizing the benefit, perceiving another's intention, appraising the value of the benefit, and so on). The two-stage information-processing model of gratitude that I introduced in *Thanks!* specifies that gratitude is the result of

(1) affirming goodness in one's life and (2) recognizing that the sources of this goodness lie at least partially outside the self. Affirmation is a signal that we have received a reward or benefit. Attributing the benefits to the intentions of others activates networks linked to social cognitive processes. The experience and expression of gratitude therefore reflect interactions between brain systems for reward evaluation and social cognition.

Dopamine is likely involved in both stages. It makes the person more sensitive to seeing rewards and attributing them to another person's good intentions. Dopamine most likely influences the person's set point to feel gratitude (along with other positive emotions). And it also influences whether the grateful feelings will motivate the person to reciprocate or "give back the goodness" in some way. Yet we must remember that relationships between neural processes and felt emotions are correlational, not causal. If reliable linkages are found, it does not mean that gratitude simply turns on dopamine or that ingratitude turns dopamine off.

What are some other reasons to have confidence in the dopamine-gratitude hypothesis? For one reason, individuals with prefrontal dysfunction (e.g., Parkinson's disease [PD]) do not display the normal benefit in mood that occurs when an individual conjures up a memory of an experience that induced gratitude. Neuroscientist Patrick McNamara and I discovered this when we asked persons with PD to recall a personal memory associated with gratitude. We also found that PD patients took longer to recall their gratitude memory and found that, in terms of length, their memories were quite a bit shorter compared to the control group. We don't know whether people who practice gratitude more frequently show any differences in brain anatomy. This also has not been specifically examined; however, brain-imaging studies reveal that the left prefrontal cortex becomes more highly active in trained meditators such as Buddhist monks. This area of the brain, as it turns out, is also associated with the experience of positive emotions such as compassion, love, and gratitude. A fascinating question would be whether the positive feelings generated by gratitude-inducing experiences might stimulate increased production or release of dopamine, thereby alleviating some of the motor and cognitive dysfunction in persons with PD.

If dopamine eventually proves to be *the* gratitude chemical, what would this mean for gratitude interventions? Would this mean that in lieu of laborious gratitude journaling one could instead opt for an injection of gratitude-juicing dopamine? Dopamine does not cross the blood-brain barrier so that option is off the table. And would we really want our gratitude to be chemically induced? Dopamine cells fire in the presence of reward for only a few seconds anyway. Although dopamine release does occur during periods of grateful feelings, there are arguments against the more radical idea that dopamine release is responsible for activating the pleasant feelings brought about when a person feels gratitude in response to the benevolence of another. Gratitude is much too complex a social-cognitive process to be reducible to neurochemistry. Nor does finding a reliable neurological mechanism for gratitude mean that some people are genetically wired for gratitude. Most important, the short-term feeling of gratitude is not the same as having a well-honed grateful disposition. As a fundamental orientation, the ability to sense the giftedness of life is a developmental achievement requiring, among other skills, the ability to reverse misfortunes, a topic needing further examination.

Here are my top ten tips for successful gratitude journaling. You will have the opportunity to systematically try these out in the twenty-one-day gratitude challenge.

TOP TEN TIPS FOR SUCCESSFUL JOURNALING

1. Take five to ten minutes to write at least every other day. Make that commitment and honor it. Choose morning or evening.

2. If you do not have a pen and paper, use the speech-recognition feature on your smartphone to record your gratitudes in the memo pad or equivalent app on your phone.

3. Seek gratitude density. Be specific. Go for depth over breadth. Give details for each entry. The journal is more than just a list of stuff.

---

4. Try to include some surprises. What unexpected blessings did you benefit from today? What were you dreading that did not happen?

5. Use the language of gifts. Think of the benefits you received today as gifts. Relish and savor the gifts you have been given.

6. Think about the people to whom you are grateful and why. Who deserves your thanks? What have you received or are receiving from them?

7. Think about and then write down those aspects of your life that you are prone to take for granted. Instead, take them as granted.

8. Let your gratitude last a long time. It is okay to repeat a blessing day after day. But do elaborate on each blessing. Give details.

9. Don't only journal about people who helped you but also about those who have helped people whom you love. We may overlook these sources of gratitude.

10. Be grateful for the negative outcomes that you avoided, escaped, prevented, or redeemed into something positive.

Beyond the Journal

Gratitude Letters and Visits

> *Silent gratitude isn't very much use to anyone.*
> —GERTRUDE STEIN[1]

Who are the people who've made a significant difference in your life? If something happened to you tomorrow, would you regret that you hadn't properly thanked these people for their role in your life?

Walter Green, successful former CEO of a major corporation, asked himself these very questions. Green was chairman of the board and CEO of Harrison Conference Services for twenty-five years, during which time it grew into the leading conference center management company in the country. After selling his business and moving to San Diego, he was ready to take on a new purpose. So he sat down and made a list of all the people who had made a major positive impact on him throughout his life. He wanted to tell these men and women how much they mattered to him before anyone's health or life was compromised and the opportunity was missed. He then spent a year traveling around the country to visit forty-four of these people to tell them how they'd made a difference in his life. During these visits, Walter conveyed his profound gratitude in a purposeful and explicit way. Walter decided to seize the moment to express his profound appreciation to these important people. He chronicled these visits in his inspirational memoir, *This Is the Moment*, and sent me a copy with the inscription, "I know you have 'mined' the subject of gratitude for many years. I thought it would interest you how I struck 'gold' on my journey."[2]

Jessica Utts, a former colleague of mine at the University of California, Davis, embarked on a similar mission. A hard-nosed statistician now at the University of California, Irvine, she developed a gratitude project for a recent milestone birthday. Sometime soon after her forty-ninth birthday she started compiling a list of the fifty most influential people in her life. These were all people she knew personally, not well-known public figures. Then for the 150 days leading up to her fiftieth birthday she spent three days on each of them, honoring them and what they had done for her. If they were still alive she sent them a card—never an e-mail—explaining what she was doing and why they were included. If they were deceased, she just spent the three days remembering them. She randomized the list (as would you expect from a statistician!) so that no one would feel as if they were first, last, or anywhere in between. In addition to the friends and relatives she tracked down, the list included teachers, the publisher who hounded her until she wrote her first book, professional colleagues, journal editors, and former students. They weren't all her favorite people, she admitted, but the most influential. All but two wrote back to her. Jessica told me that "it will come as no surprise to you to know that it benefited me more than it did any of the recipients!"

* THERE'S NOTHING LIKE A GRATITUDE VISIT *

Walter and Jessica discovered up close and personally what researchers have now learned through controlled clinical trials. One of the most effective ways to deepen your own gratefulness is to write a letter of gratitude to an important person in your life whom you've never properly taken the time to thank and then visit that person to present him or her with the letter. Studies published in the most rigorous scientific publications show that the gratitude visit can increase happiness and decrease depression in the letter writer for as long as three months after the visit!

In most of the studies on gratitude journaling I have conducted, I did not distinguish between felt and expressed gratitude. My goal in those studies was getting people to feel grateful by recognizing the sources of goodness in their lives. Yet an emotion such as gratitude has many components from whatever elicits it to our bodily reactions, to the way we feel about it, to what we do to express it. Emotions yearn to be expressed. The word *emotion* comes from the Latin *movere*, meaning *to move*. Emotions move us to do things. When we are angry, we are moved to strike out. When we are afraid, we are motivated to flee. Love moves us to embrace. Prides causes us to celebrate. And so on.

Expression may be an especially critical aspect of gratitude. The concept of *thanksgiving* implies that thanks are being given to someone. When we feel grateful, we want to express that thanks to either the person who has gifted us or more generally by passing on the goodness we have received to others. The expressions of gratitude go beyond a simple tit-for-tat reciprocity. Gratitude felt can even inspire great acts of charity and philanthropy. J. David Wimberly was so moved by his wife's care at Brigham and Women's Hospital in Cambridge, Massachusetts, that he created the J. David and Virginia Wimberly Professorship in Neurology at Harvard Medical School. The following year, he continued his generosity with a $500,000 gift to Harvard Medical School to help advance the Alzheimer's Biomarkers Discovery Program, which is collecting samples from hundreds of patients in order to identify specific biological traits of the disease. If detected early enough researchers believe the disease's onset can be prevented or delayed, a noble goal given the rising incidence of the disease in the aging population.

By contrast, not expressing gratitude can leave a lingering sense of discomfort. Famed humanistic psychologist Abraham Maslow discussed the importance of expressing gratitude toward a benefactor and the psychological tension that results when we don't express thanks to people to whom we feel a positive sense of indebtedness. Toward the end of his career he wrote, "It is vital that people 'count their blessings': to appreciate what they possess without having to undergo its actual loss." He even offered a practice for accomplishing this:

> One method is to imagine that someone you care about might die—or will die—soon. Think as vividly as you can how you would feel, what you would truly lose, and about how you would be sorry. Would you have any regret or remorse? How would you conduct an effective goodbye to avoid later feeling a sense of gnawing incompleteness? And, how would you best preserve your fullest memory of this person?[3]

This might seem like a depressing exercise but try it in your gratitude journal. What if people were asked to communicate explicitly their appreciation toward a significant other? What might the effects be of a "gratitude confrontation"?

Evidence that gratitude visits can make a measureable difference comes from Martin Seligman's positive psychology laboratory at the University of Pennsylvania. Seligman and his colleagues gave participants one week to write a letter of gratitude and then deliver it in person. The instructions stated the following:

> Select one important person from your past who has made a major positive difference in your life and to whom you have never fully expressed your thanks. Choose someone who is still alive. Write a testimonial just long enough to cover one laminated page. Take your time composing this—several weeks if required. Invite that person to your home or travel to that person's home. It is important that

you do this face to face, not just in writing or on the phone. Do not tell the person the purpose of the visit in advance.

Bring a laminated version of your testimonial with you as a gift. Read your testimonial aloud slowly, with expression and eye contact. Then let the other person react unhurriedly. Reminisce together about the concrete events that make this person so important to you.[4]

What was the effect of composing and delivering the letter for those who participated in the experiment? When their moods were measured after one week of doing the assigned exercise, participants were happier and less depressed. This boost in happiness and decrease in depressive symptoms were maintained at follow-up assessments one week and one month later.[5] It turns out that a gratitude visit is one of the exercises that, to Seligman's surprise (he once confided to me, "Bob, I don't do gratitude"), made people lastingly less depressed and happier than any other positive psychology intervention.

The benefits of gratitude visits extend beyond what we have observed for the gratitude journaling practice. It may not be practical for you to schedule a formal gratitude visit on a regular basis but most people can make time every day to express their appreciation to someone who provides a service—the postal worker, UPS driver, your daughter's soccer coach, pharmacist, and so on would love to hear from you. Maybe it is an author who has inspired you. Maybe it is someone who has inspired your own vision of what matters in life. Be creative and think of specific individuals who have benefitted you materially,

54   GRATITUDE WORKS!

emotionally, or intangibly. Use the method described in the Seligman experiment and write that person a letter and, if possible, visit and read the letter out loud in person, on either a special day (birthday, anniversary, or holiday) or a random one. If it is not someone whom you personally know, e-mail them your letter. Describe in detail what he or she did for you and exactly how it affected your life; mention how you often remember his or her efforts. Some people find it uplifting to write gratitude letters to individuals whom they don't know personally but who have influenced their lives (such as authors or politicians) or those who made their lives safer or healthier (such as their doctors, auto mechanics, or local police).

One of the participants in Seligman's study, a graduate student in chemical engineering, wrote a testimonial to her dad, recalling special things he had done or said to her over the years and how he had been a role model in helping her to become a better person. For example, he taught her humility by serving lunch and drinks and snacks to laborers who worked in their yard. On the flight to her college orientation, he ordered the same vegan meal she had though he himself was not a vegetarian. She recalled how he always patiently bore with her mood swings and was always there for her, arms open wide, always genuinely happy to see her.

It would be disingenuous for me to suggest that there is always a happy ending to these encounters. The experience did not turn out so well for one Finnish participant who paid a visit to a former teacher. She crafted a heartfelt letter and made an appointment to visit with him. Noticing his fidgetiness during her reading of the letter to him, she waited for his response. Much to her embarrassment, he thought that she had an ulterior motive—that the whole meeting was a ruse to get something from him. The entire experience was humiliating for her. Many of us unfortunately don't always know how to be gracious *receivers* of others' gratitude. We hide our role as giver or we minimize the gift. Instead of validating the thank-you with a kind "you're welcome," we say, "think nothing of it," "it was nothing," "don't mention it," or "not a problem," as we dismiss it. But don't let that deter you. The odds are much more likely that the recipient will be touched—and thank you in return.

* THE ART AND SCIENCE OF LETTER WRITING *

Recently, there's been a surge of interest in the once feeble domain of letter writing as a vehicle for improving health. Phil Watkins, one of the central figures in gratitude research, conducted a study that examined mood changes as the result of writing a letter of gratitude, among other activities.[6] His findings revealed that writing a gratitude letter produced a greater increase in happiness compared to other gratitude-increasing methods such as gratitude journaling and recalling past events for which the person was grateful. In another recent study, participants were asked to pray and write letters to God. Both prayer and the letters increased personal insight and positive emotions, including gratitude. The authors explained that the act of praying or explaining to another (in this case in a letter to God) improved the participants' positive feelings about life events.

Researchers at Kent State University have systematically explored the influence of prolonged writing, or writing multiple letters over time, as a means to better understand how expressing gratitude affects happiness. Every two weeks for an eight-week period, three undergraduate classes of students wrote one letter to people who had had a positive influence on their lives. As part of the experiment's design, three other randomly selected classes (the control group) did not write these gratitude letters. The participants did not mail the letters or make the gratitude visit as they did in the Seligman studies. They typed or handwrote three letters of gratitude (other research showed that writing by hand or computer makes no significant difference). What matters most is expressive writing with a focus on meaningful content. The "what" matters much more than the "how." Participants were instructed to avoid trivial letters (e.g., thank-you notes for material gifts or "thanks for saying hello to me this morning" kinds of things) and to compose substantial letters that acknowledged something significant for which they felt gratitude toward the recipient. Participants were instructed to be reflective, write expressively, and compose letters from a positive orientation. The expressive writing intervention was limited to three letters to avoid "overpracticing" or inducing a "gratitude fatigue effect."

Previous research focused on a single letter whereas this investigation was the first to examine multiple letters over time. The results showed that multiple letters produced a beneficial cumulative effect for happiness and gratitude. Just three installments of ten to fifteen minutes (average writing time for

35 percent of the sample) and one page in length (53 percent of the sample) were sufficient to usher in positive change. After each letter was written, the students took a survey that gauged their mood, their satisfaction with life, and their feelings of gratitude and happiness. According to researcher Steven Toepfer, the students' levels of happiness increased after each letter and 75 percent of them said they wanted to keep writing the letters, even when the study was finished.[7]

This suggests that as an intentional activity, writing letters of gratitude can yield important benefits in a relatively short period of time. The preexisting and often silent resource of gratitude can be mobilized in the pursuit of not only happiness but also toward the growth of gratitude and ultimately overall well-being.

Another study by Toepfer and his students examined the effects of a similar, sustained letters of gratitude writing campaign on levels of depression and physical symptoms (aches and pains). The positive and insightful writing that is a hallmark of the gratitude letter was associated with many outcomes including health improvements. Results indicated that those who wrote letters over time experienced less depression compared to nonwriters. Perhaps writing letters of gratitude is a way to reduce depressive symptoms and improve physical health, including psychosomatic illness.[8]

Why Letter Writing Works

Although we know that writing a letter often makes us feel good, what does psychological research have to tell us about why the experiments we just reviewed have such a strong effect? For one thing, research has shown that translating thoughts into concrete language has advantages over just thinking the thoughts. We think much faster than we can write or speak. When you put your thoughts into words, either out loud or on paper, the thinking process is slowed down. It makes the thoughts more real, more concrete, and helps us to elaborate on them. When I take the time to write a letter of gratitude, writing gives me time to reflect on the person's many acts of kindness toward me in a manner that would not occur if I just thought about them or even if I hastily spoke a few words of thanks. Over time, spoken or written thanks can actually produce long-term changes in a person's overall levels of gratitude. Research has shown that grateful people have a particular linguistic style that uses the language of gifts, givers, blessings, blessed, fortune, fortunate, and abundance. Less grateful people are preoccupied with burdens, curses, deprivations, and complaints, and their words reflect this negative focus. Writing enables us to traffic in the language of thankfulness in a manner that begins to shape our reality. We begin to see more gifts and blessings and fewer burdens and curses.

Something else happens when we put feelings into words. Our brain actually begins to change. Recent neuroimaging studies suggest the possibility of a gratitude-driven neuroplasticity. A number of studies have demonstrated that talking about an emotional image produces less activity in the region of the brain (the amygdala) associated with processing unpleasant emotions compared to just viewing the same image without speaking. When people see a photograph of an angry or fearful face, the activity in the amygdala increases, which serves as an alarm to activate a cascade of biological systems to protect the body in times of danger. Scientists see a robust amygdala response even when they show emotional photographs so quickly that a person can't even register them. Seeing an angry face and calling it an angry face actually changes our brain response. In a study conducted by researchers at the University of California, Los Angeles, thirty people viewed images of individuals making different emotional expressions.[9] Below the picture of the face they either saw two words, such as *angry* or *fearful*, and chose which emotion described the face, or they saw two names, such as *Harry* and *Sally*, and chose the gender-appropriate name that matched the face. When participants attached the word *angry*, there was a diminished response in the amygdala but when they attached the name *Harry*, there was no such reduction, proving it was emotional labeling, not labeling per se that was responsible for the effect on the brain.

Putting feelings into words can make a person feel better because doing so dampens activity in the parts of the brain associated with negativity. When you say how you feel happy, angry, or grateful, you disrupt the affective responses in the brain that would otherwise occur if you just looked at the emotional image silently. So the effectiveness of extensive writing in a journal, penning a gratitude letter, or otherwise devising a means to put your grateful thoughts into grateful language may depend on neural machinery that neuroscience is beginning to unravel.

Giving Thanks Through Testimony

Journaling and letter writing are activities that are carried out in private but the irony is that gratitude is a social emotion that is experienced in the context of relationships. These journals and letters that we write are testimonies to others of what are meaningful sources of gratitude to us. We intend these to be shared. And this is why they are so powerful. We are social creatures by nature. We were created with a longing for belonging, an urge to merge with others. There are many different forms and expressions of testimonies.

There are secular and religious rituals centered on the giving of thanks. Every culture has special rituals and traditions for expressing thanksgiving. Harvest festivals provide specific occasions to recognize that life's gifts are something we receive. Within Judaism, for example, the proper response to divine gifts is a public proclamation of praise and thanksgiving for God's steadfast love and faithfulness. There is a strong communal aspect to expressions of thanksgiving to God, in which public testimony calls attention to the grace of God in the life of the believer. This declaration is the testimonial function of gratitude that serves to draw in and incorporate a larger community in joyful celebration of what has happened in one's life and experience. One classic praise testimony, popular in the contemporary African American church, goes something like this: "Thank you, God, for waking me up this morning; for putting shoes on my feet, clothes on my back, and food on my table. Thank you, God, for health and strength and the activities of my limbs. Thank you that I awoke this morning clothed in my right mind."[10]

In testimony, believers describe what God has done in their lives in biblical and personal words, and the testifier's community affirms them in some way. At their Thanksgiving Day service, a megachurch that I have attended has the tradition of passing the microphone so that the faithful can share their testimonies of how God has performed miracles in their lives. It is an amazing time. The spirit of thankfulness is palpable in the auditorium. Tears flow freely. At the same time, there is nothing unusual or out of the ordinary about these testimonies. This is a ritual that is repeated around the globe weekly in times of corporate praise and proclamations of thanksgiving.

The Perfect Thank-You

A few years ago, *Reader's Digest* magazine asked me to comment on a thank-you letter in light of what the elements of an "ideal" thank-you would look like. They asked me to respond to a letter that former president George H. W. Bush wrote to the actress Goldie Hawn in which he expressed his thanks to her for her company at a dinner:

> Dear Goldie,
>   Am I enchanted? You bet. Thanks for giving me such a relaxed good time at dinner.
>   When Jane Weintraub told me where I was sitting, I was a little worried only because I'm not too hot of a dinner partner. (I didn't ask you to dance—on that one, look at it this way—you've still got 2 good feet.) Anyway, you were a fantastic dinner partner. You made me feel welcome and

totally at ease. I didn't even have to unveil my 12-point plan
for dealing with Gorbachev. Thanks for being so darn nice!!
    Good luck—
    George Bush[11]

I'm no Emily Post when it comes to etiquette. Besides, I
thought it rather presumptuous for me to comment on the
actions of a former commander-in-chief. Nevertheless, I proceeded as instructed and my analysis was that he did all the
right things: (1) President Bush's self-deprecating humor
deflected attention from himself, (2) he put the focus where it
rightly belongs, on the source of his gratitude, and (3) the
former president mentioned specific benefits that Goldie
Hawn provided, avoiding the all-too-common "thanks-for-
everything" approach.

* THANKS IN THE WORKPLACE *

*At Whole Foods we practice appreciations at the end of all of
our meetings, including even our board meetings—voluntarily
expressing gratitude and thanks to our coworkers for the
thoughtful and helpful things they do for us. It would be hard
to overestimate how powerful appreciations have been at
Whole Foods as a transformational practice for releasing more
love throughout the company.*
    —JOHN MACKEY, CEO OF WHOLE FOODS MARKET[12]

As part of National Thank-You Week a few years ago, research
revealed that British businesses were split between "thankers"
and "thank-nots." The thankers were those workplace leaders

who recognize the importance of appreciating and motivating their employees, and the thank-nots were leaders who neglect to do so. When asked whether they thought UK bosses were better or worse at saying thank-you now than ten years before, 22 percent of those surveyed thought they had improved but 37 percent felt they had grown worse. Some good news was that the percentage of people in full- or part-time work in the United Kingdom who never receive a thank-you had halved in the past year, falling from one in three (30 percent) to one in six (16 percent). However, although half (51 percent) of the working population receive a thank-you once a month or more, only slightly fewer—44 percent—receive a thank-you just once every few months or less frequently. Moira Clark, professor of strategic marketing and director of the Henley Centre for Customer Management at the University of Reading, comments, "Great staff are the only competitive advantage any organization has that cannot be copied so it is vital that employees are made to feel appreciated and valued. My own research substantiates this, revealing that in high-performing companies, that is, those with high customer retention levels, staff are frequently rewarded, in other words, thanked. However, in low-performing companies, employees are punished, e.g., ignored or reprimanded, more frequently than they are rewarded."[13]

The survey also revealed that more people left their last job because they didn't feel valued or appreciated by management than for an improved work-life balance or pay check. Just over two in five (43 percent) people said that not feeling valued contributed greatly or a fair amount to their decision to leave compared with three in ten (34 percent) who left searching for a better work-life balance. With the cost of replacing an employee estimated at almost $13,000, consistent, genuine gratitude is a cost-effective policy.[14]

Fast Company blogger Howard Jacobson writes, "Almost everyone I know, from pastors to parents, from cashiers to carpet cleaners, from architects to accountants, suffers from GDD: Gratitude Deficit Disorder. Despite all our good intentions and actions, we receive much more flak than gratitude. We are hungry for genuine appreciation and thanks. We want to know that we matter, that our efforts are making the world a better place."[15] Effective leaders have always known that being thanked and appreciated for hard work has a really positive effect, making employees feel happier, work harder, and stay with the company longer. Taking the time to say a personal thank-you for a job well done costs nothing yet can make a big contribution to the productivity and success of a business. Being thanked has a slightly greater effect on morale than on productivity and retention, with almost nine out of ten people saying a thank-you has a positive or very positive effect on morale compared with eight out of ten for productivity and retention.

Gratitude Pays Off

Did you ever notice when the server scrawls a big thank-you across your dining check or doodles a happy face alongside it? There is a reason for it. Restaurant bills on which the server writes "thank you" produce tips that are as much as 11 percent higher than do bills without an expression of gratitude.[16] Also, including thank-you notes in mail surveys typically increases response rates. In one study, active customers of a single jewelry store who received a telephone call to thank them for their business spent more in the store during the next month than customers who were not called. Interestingly, the customers who were called to be thanked also spent more than customers who received a call to thank them for their business *and* to announce that the store would be having a 20 percent off sale during the next two months.[17] We don't respond as well when thank-yous have strings attached. Marketers know that gratitude is good for business but more so when it wells up spontaneously in consumers. People don't want to be pressured into expressions of gratitude. One study of Texas wineries (not an oxymoron) found that the higher the visitor's feelings of gratitude while at a winery, the more money they spent on wine and souvenirs in the tasting room.[18]

According to research from Louisiana State University, saying "thank you" goes a long way toward shaping public opinion—and can even affect a state's economy. Randy Raggio and Judith Anne Garretson Folse, two marketing professors at Louisiana State University, studied two thank-you campaigns that ran nationwide in the wake of Hurricanes Katrina and Rita. One campaign, sponsored by the Louisiana Office of Tourism, comprised a series of television spots; the other, a grassroots effort, included a "Louisiana Thanks You!" message on ninety billboards and in radio spots. In two online surveys, conducted in April 2006 and November 2006, respondents who had seen or heard a thank-you ad had more positive attitudes toward Louisiana than those who hadn't. In fact, every ten exposures to a thank-you ad equated to a 1.5 percent increase in a respondent's willingness to travel to Louisiana over other states. "Most ads lose their impact after eight to twelve exposures, but not these," said Raggio.[19]

* MAKING GRATEFUL KIDS *

Jeffrey Froh, psychologist at Hofstra University out on Long Island, New York, is a former school psychologist who is now a research professor and *the* worldwide expert on teaching kids to think gratefully. He claims that his son wrote his first thank-you note at the age of six months. Okay, so he exaggerates a bit. Given the difficulty in getting our kids to write thank-yous, starting as soon as possible is not a bad idea. Why wait? The practice of gratitude should begin early. We do teach our children relentlessly to say "thank you." Do you remember all the time you spent prompting your preschoolers with "what do you say?" Notwithstanding Jeff's son, most children don't manage to produce "thank you" spontaneously until sometime between the ages of four and six. A study in England asked parents to draw up a list of the most desirable children's manners learned at the table. "Thank you" was at the top of the list.[20]

Along with colleagues Giacomo Bono and Alex Wood, Froh and I designed an experiment in which elementary school classes of eight- to eleven-year-olds were randomly assigned to a gratitude curriculum in which they were trained to think about the intentions of someone who had provided them with a benefit in ways that have been shown to foster deeper gratitude and appreciation of the giver's efforts. The instructions read as follows:

> Pretend that you were out sick from school for an entire week. Your friend knows that you have been out sick, so he goes to your house to bring you his notes and any assignments you have missed while you were out. In this example, your friend went out of his way to help you on purpose. He did not accidentally come over to your house. He thought about how you have not been to school and needed your school work, so he intentionally helped you by bringing you your assignments.[21]

In a subsequent session, they were trained to think about the cost incurred by the person who provided a benefit:

> Can anyone tell me what the word *cost* means? Just like we learned last week, when someone intentionally helps us, they also give something up to help us. A possible example may include: "your sister helps you to do your homework and by helping you she gives up some of her time doing her own homework." In this example, what did your sister give

up? Possible answers may include her time doing her homework, her knowledge, and her help.[22]

A second classroom of students of the same age was assigned to an attention-control curriculum in which they focused on topics that were emotionally neutral and unassociated with beneficial interpersonal exchanges. Students in both groups read vignettes depicting three different helping situations. They were instructed to imagine they were the main character in the stories. Following each story, students were asked four questions. The questions for each vignette were tailored to the respective benefactor (i.e., sister, friend, and parent) and situation (i.e., help studying, lending cleats to play soccer, and sharing the computer). We attempted to measure all three grateful cognitions across all three vignettes. Using "sister" as an example, the questions about a sister helping with homework were as follows:

- "How much did your sister help you on purpose?" (aims to measure intent)
- "How much did your sister give up to help you?" (aims to measure cost)
- "How much did your sister (quizzing) you help you?"

The students in the gratitude group also read *The Giving Tree* by Shel Silverstein. This classic book about a tree that starts out as a leafy playground, shade provider, and apple bearer for a rambunctious little boy and ends up making many sacrifices for him was used to further illustrate the role of intentionality and cost in gratitude.

The teachers who participated in the study then gave their students the opportunity to draw a picture or write a letter as an expression of gratitude to the parent-teacher association (PTA) for their presentation. All teachers read the following instructions to their students on returning to their classrooms after the presentation:

> The presentation you just saw was given by our Parent Teacher Association. We have about 5 minutes of free time. You can either use this time to write a "thank you" card to the PTA using the paper provided or you can just hang out. Some people like to say "thank you" by writing something or drawing a picture. So if you choose to write the thank you card, feel free to either write a letter or draw a picture using either a pen, pencil, crayon or marker. If you choose to write the "thank you" card, please be sure to print your first and last name at the bottom so they know who the card is coming from, and I'll pass them on to the PTA.[23]

After the activity was over, the teachers collected the pictures and letters and identified the students who participated by circling their names on a class roster. The teachers then gave the pictures and letters to the building-level school psychologist to mail to the PTA. We found that the children who had been in the gratitude curriculum wrote 80 percent more thank-you cards to their PTA than the control group. Their teachers even observed them to be happier and more giving compared to those in the control group. This demonstrates clearly that we can teach children to become more aware of the costs and intentions of those who help them and cultivate the habit of expressing gratitude.

In another study, eighty-nine children and adolescents were randomly assigned to either write or not write a gratitude letter. They were asked to "think of the people—parents, friends, coaches, teammates, and so on—who have been especially kind to you but whom you have never properly thanked. Choose one person you could meet individually for a face-to-face meeting in the next week. Your task is to write a gratitude letter (a letter of thanks) to this individual and deliver it in person." Students in the control group were given the following instructions: "Expressing your feelings is a good thing to do. Think about yesterday. Write about some of the things you did and what you felt like when you were doing these things."

Here is an excerpt from a seventeen-year-old female student's gratitude letter to her mother:

> I would like to take this time to thank you for all that you do
> on a daily basis and have been doing my whole life . . . I am
> so thankful that I get to drive in with you [to school] every
> day and that you listen and care about the things going on in
> our lives. I also want to thank you for all the work you do
> for our church. Every week you work to provide a great
> lineup of worship that allows everyone to enter in and glorify
> God every Sunday . . . I thank you for being there whenever
> I need you. I thank you that when the world is against me

that you stand up for me and you are my voice when I can't speak for myself. I thank you for caring about my life and wanting to be involved. I thank you for the words of encouragement and hugs of love that get me through every storm. I thank you for sitting through countless games in the cold and rain and still having the energy to make dinner and all the things you do . . . I am so blessed to have you as my mommy and I have no idea what I would have done without you. I love you a million hugs and kisses.

Students were given ten to fifteen minutes daily for five days to either write their gratitude letter or journal about daily events. Findings indicated that youth who initially scored low in happiness reported greater gratitude and happiness after the research project as well as at the two-month follow-up. This was a powerful finding because youth who are high in positive emotions are more intrinsically motivated, think more critically and flexibly, are more active planners, and monitor their own learning. Their unhappy peers, in contrast, tend to be disengaged from school, withdrawing from and resisting activities and people associated with it.[24]

In today's social media age, letter writing is likely to be viewed as an arcane relic from the past. How can youth become engaged in such a seemingly obsolete practice? For them to buy in to any of these ideas, it is essential that any gratitude practice be made fun and exciting. For example, when practicing as a school psychologist, Froh recalls an art teacher giving a gifted student with Asperger syndrome art supplies to use during counseling (drawing reduced his stress). Instead of saying "thank you" or writing a thank-you letter and reading it in person to his teacher, he drew a cartoon character offering a colorful bouquet of flowers and gave it to her in person. Had traditional gratitude expression been pushed onto him, he might have ignored or had been uncommunicative about his teacher's kindness, and she might have perceived him as ungrateful. Because of adult encouragement, support, and openness, he was able to say thanks in a way that was enjoyable, creative, and rewarding.[25]

* IT DOESN'T MATTER HOW LONG IT TAKES *

When you become aware that someone has made an uncommon sacrifice on your behalf, go and thank them. Even if it takes some time. Former surgeon general of the United States C. Everett Koop recalls this about his youngest patient: "One day at Children's Hospital I got a phone call from a nearby hospital about a dying newborn with a diaphragmatic hernia. I drove there at breakneck speed. I ran up to the ninth floor and ran back down." By the time Koop placed the baby on the table, the little boy was blue and lifeless. "With no time for sterile precautions, I opened his chest and massaged his tiny heart with my finger until it began to beat. Then I finished the operation," he wrote.

About twenty-five years later Koop's secretary ushered a strapping six-foot-four-inch young man into the office. "My father thought you'd like to meet me," he told Koop. "You operated on me when I was fifty-five minutes old." Koop ran around his desk and hugged him.[26]

It is a wonderful feeling to be the recipient of someone's heartfelt thanksgiving. The effect of expressed gratitude on the receiver has not been systematically studied by scientists but we all know what it is like for our efforts to be acknowledged by others. It feels great to receive thanks but we should not expect it. Imagine if Koop were waiting in his office all those years for his former patient to return. "Blessed are those who can give without remembering and take without forgetting," said the British poet and author Elizabeth Bibesco.[27] Gratitude may be the memory of the heart but generosity is the forgetfulness of the giver.

Growing Gratitude Through Spiritual Disciplines

When traveling on vacation, I find that I am often drawn to reading books on the spiritual disciplines. I'm not sure why, but I think I use them as a counterpoint to the free-form, somewhat indulgent nature of travel. On a recent trip to Disneyworld, I took along my copy of Dallas Willard's classic *The Spirit of the Disciplines*,[1] plus two downloaded additional books on spiritual practices just in case these disciplines were really put to the test en route to the Magic Kingdom. A professor of philosophy at the University of Southern California, Willard has had worldwide influence through his writings and teachings on how to grow in the "fruit of the spirit," namely love, joy, peace, patience, kindness, goodness, faithfulness, gentleness, and self-control (Galatians 5:22–23). Growth occurs through the intentional spiritual disciplines of prayer, fellowship, service, study, simplicity, chastity, solitude, and fasting, as well as others.

What is a discipline? It is an activity, according to Willard, that "is within our power—something we can do—that brings us to a point where we can do what we at present cannot do by direct effort."[2] The word *discipline* as translated in the New Testament is a Greek word, *gumnasia*, from which we get the English words *gymnasium* and *gymnastics*, both of which imply the pursuit of growth through disciplined exercise. Spiritual disciplines are exercises. Without the discipline of exercise, we cannot grow. Everything from learning a language to writing a book to swimming the two-hundred-meter individual medley in the Olympics requires it.

When you hear the word *discipline*, you may have many associations, not all of them positive. No one likes to be disciplined if it means being punished for disobedience. We bristle at the thought of someone disciplining us, perhaps recalling unpleasant memories of being sent to the principal's office (or worse, the office of the vice principal). Nor may you want to be thought of as a *disciple*, the term conjuring up images of a person who needs to be taught what to do or think. Discipline as discussed here indicates strength of character. A disciple is simply a person who chooses to draw humbly and gratefully on the wisdom of the historic practical steps and exercises to make things happen today that would not otherwise happen without a rigorous practice. It is all good.

In *The Spirit of the Disciplines*, Dallas Willard identified fifteen different spiritual disciplines, but he didn't mention gratitude. Some years ago I had the fortuitous opportunity to be seated next to him during a luncheon at a professional conference, so I asked him where he thought gratitude fits in. Pausing between bites, Willard, who is a Southern Baptist, gave my question some serious reflection and answered, "Celebration. Gratitude is about celebration." We engage in celebration, he told me, when we receive life and all its gifts with enjoyment as we dwell on the greatness of who God is and what he has done for us. "Holy delight and joy is the great antidote to despair and is a wellspring of genuine gratitude," writes Willard in *The Spirit of the Disciplines*.[3] Celebration is also what the great teacher of gratitude Brother David Steindl-Rast identifies as the core of gratefulness. By celebration he means "an act of heightened and focused intellectual and emotional appreciation."[4] I love this definition. We receive a gift, we recognize its worth, and we appreciate its value. Our intellectual focus is sharpened, and our emotional response intensifies in the act of (spontaneous or deliberate, but in either case willing) appreciation, which we call gratitude.

GATEWAYS TO GRATITUDE

All religions have spiritual practices that have been handed down through the centuries. Buddhists burn incense and meditate. Muslims face Mecca and submit five times daily on their prayer rugs. Faithful Jews keep kosher. Christians memorize scripture and build small groups. There are so many practices from so many varied traditions that we certainly cannot do them all well, so we will consider only a handful that I believe are especially helpful in cultivating a grateful way of life.

The link between spiritual practices and the practice of gratitude is long and historic. Gratitude is a universal religious sentiment, evident in the thanks offerings described in ancient scriptures and in traditional hymns and contemporary praise and worship choruses. Cultivating gratitude through spiritual disciplines has almost universally been seen as a hallmark of spiritual maturity in all the great religious traditions. I have thought about how a few of these practices can make an important contribution to our growing in gratitude, particularly in the way they can help us overcome obstacles to living gratefully. In the Christian tradition, spiritual disciplines not only help a person overcome ingrained bad habits but they also help believers receive the grace of God. Grace is unmerited favor. The word *gratitude* is derived from the Latin *gratia*, meaning grace, graciousness, or gratefulness. All derivatives from this Latin root have to do with kindness, generousness, gifts, the beauty of giving and receiving, or getting something for nothing. For Christians, without an awareness of God's grace, it is impossible to cultivate gratitude. And practices are what make a person more sensitive to moments of grace. In this chapter, I discuss how practices not typically associated with developing gratitude (fasting, solitude and silence, simplicity, and confession) may be especially effective. There are many other disciplines, of course, but I have chosen to focus on some that have been overlooked. Just as different methods of journaling are more or less effective for different people, you will find that you may be drawn to a particular discipline and not to others. That is fine. Start with what you think you need the most. In the "Trying It Out" boxes, I offer specific suggestions for practicing each discipline.

Fasting

Next time you watch television take note of the number of commercials about food. My own informal survey during the 2012 summer Olympics revealed that approximately one-half of all ads are about food, most often for fast-food restaurants. When you add to that the proliferation of reality shows centered on cooking challenges or restaurant makeovers, it seems we are obsessed with food and eating. A recent study found that in 96 half-hour blocks of preschool programming on Nickelodeon, the Disney Channel, and Cartoon Network there were a total of 130 food-related advertisements. Exposure to this bombardment of ads is often implicated in increasing obesity rates, but what interests me more is their impact on our ability to feel and express gratitude.

Fasting, the practice of voluntarily giving up food and sometimes drink for a significant period of time, is a discipline with a long history in many of the world's religious traditions. It is a given in Judaism, for example, ten days after the New Year celebration, and in Islam during the month of Ramadan. To be sure, food is one of the great blessings of God in our lives, a true pleasure and a true necessity. Gratitude journals that I have collected frequently reveal the blessings of food; respondents have listed things such as "a hot meal," "a new recipe," "enjoyed my turkey burger," "yummy bacon." But temporarily depriving oneself of food and drink can foster a deeper and sustained gratefulness.

People fast for many spiritual reasons, including to strengthen their prayer lives, to seek God's guidance, to seek deliverance or protection, to humble oneself, to seek repentance, to overcome temptations, and to express love and worship to God. Fasting can also have a variety of psychological, spiritual, and health benefits. Recent research has even found that regular fasting can protect against certain brain diseases, including Alzheimer's and Parkinson's.[5] But it is not typically seen as a way of building gratitude. Why not? The one billion or so Muslims around the world who fast during Ramadan become acutely aware of the unlimited abundance of divine favor that God Almighty has blessed humanity with, particularly with regards to sustenance. The cultivation of gratitude is a core purpose of Islam, and few spiritual practices cultivate gratitude as does intentionally fasting during Ramadan. Muslims fast to give thanks to the Almighty for his blessings and to force reliance on him. The prophet Muhammad fasted regularly, sometimes for months on end, and advised his followers to fast outside of the obligatory month of Ramadan.

Fasting can also reveal just how much time and energy we devote to food and eating, which affects our ability to devote ourselves to spiritual growth. Fasting shifts our attention and orients us in a different way. Some have said that it is the most important of all the disciplines, and one of the most overlooked. Describing her own struggles with keeping fasts, author Lauren Winner writes in *Mudhouse Sabbath* that fasting accomplishes a repositioning of the mind, a realization that we depend on others for sustenance, whereas a state of satiation leaves us with an illusion of self-reliance. One Jewish guide to fasting states that "at the heart of this practice is a desire to shift our attention away from our immediate needs and to focus on more spiritual concerns."[6] Once you are able to regularly practice fasting, you will find that you can tolerate all sorts of other kinds of deprivations. Fasting is helpful in developing gratitude because when we fast we learn that it's possible for us to have unfulfilled desires and still survive. It also sharpens our ability to be grateful for food in general and to savor the rich panoply of smells, sights, and flavors in the specialness of the first meal coming off a fast.

Why is occasional fasting a surefire way to spark gratitude? My research interviews with people from a wide variety of backgrounds and life experiences lead me to conclude that an authentic, deeply held sense of gratefulness toward life requires some degree of deprivation. We cannot recognize some blessings until they are lost. When we lose—or perceive a threat of loss—to some aspect of life, we may see other aspects of life as more precious. We have all heard of people who have narrowly escaped a brush with death, only to come back supercharged to embrace all of the possibilities that life offers. Through the process of appreciation, what was once taken for granted is now seen as special. There is nothing quite like the potential unavailability of something (or someone) to make us value it more. Psychologists call this the "principle of scarcity"—assigning greater value to opportunities when they are less available.

Professor Michael Zigarelli of Messiah College has found that there is a positive relationship between periodic fasting and gratitude. He reports that people who have higher levels of gratitude are much more likely to fast regularly than are those who score lower on a standard measure of gratitude. That doesn't necessarily indicate a cause-and-effect relationship. It may be that gratitude leads a person to engage in periodic fasts, or that the two are correlated but not causative. Nevertheless, these are the first data that indicate a link between the discipline of fasting and increased gratitude.[7] The proverbial "more research is needed" applies here.

TRYING IT OUT

- Make a decision to fast for the purpose of increasing your gratitude.
- If you are new to fasting, start with one meal rather than an entire day.
- Use the time you would use to prepare, eat, and clean up after meals to reflect on the gifts that you received today.
- Estimate how much money you saved on meals and donate that money to a food bank or other charity that serves people less fortunate than yourself.
- Stay in a prayerful attitude throughout the day. Transform physical hunger into spiritual hunger.

Silence and Solitude

There is a story of a former CEO of a major corporation who, at the age of fifty-nine, tires of the cutthroat rat race and desires a simpler, gentler life. He joins a monastery and takes a vow of silence in which he is allowed to say only two words every seven years. After the first seven years, the abbot calls him in and asks if he would like to say anything. "Bed hard," he says. The abbot nods and whisks him away. Seven more years pass. The abbot brings him back in and asks for his two words. He clears his throats and says, "food bad." The head abbot nods and sends him away. Seven more years pass. Once again he appears before the abbot. "Do you have anything to say?" asks the abbot. "I quit," he says. "That's not surprising," replied the abbot. "You've done nothing but complain ever since you got here."

Silence and solitude give us plenty of time to focus on what is going wrong in our lives, but used fruitfully, they can spur a greater awareness of the giftedness of life. As practiced, the two work best when they are combined. Although not all silence is solitude, silence is always a part of solitude. Silence, complete quiet for spiritual purposes, can be one of the most difficult disciplines to develop because we may have few opportunities to have it in a world where it seems that we are never anywhere without sound. But silence is one of the most valuable practices for cultivating the interior life. These disciplines are often discussed together in various religious traditions, so I will consider them together as one practice.

Beloved teacher and theologian Henri Nouwen wrote, "Without solitude it is virtually impossible to live a spiritual life."[8] The devotional writer Richard Foster says that solitude is more a state of mind and heart than it is a place.[9] You don't literally have to be alone to be in solitude. There is solitude of the heart that can be maintained at all times. Crowds, or lack of them, have little to do with this kind of inward attentiveness. That's a good thing because it is impractical for most of us, most of the time, to simply retreat from humanity. Similarly, Buddhists distinguish solitude of the body from solitude of the mind. Physical solitude is what we are all familiar with. Mental solitude entails quietness, a stilling of the mind and tongue. Getting away from everyone else is not a necessary condition for mental solitude. A person can experience mental solitude while in the presence of others, such as when you are "alone" in the company of strangers or when an intimate couple goes away to foster togetherness. In these cases, a person consciously chooses to disengage from the demands of social interaction without being aloof or rude. It is maintaining one's own space and not getting caught up in a typhoon of social activity.

Viewed from the lens of psychological science, solitude presents a paradox. Deep within us reside the needs for attachment, affiliation, and sociality, yet people still want to spend time in solitude. Why is that? The *Oxford English Dictionary* defines *solitude* primarily as "the state of being or living alone; loneliness; seclusion; solitariness (of persons)."[10] But solitude is far different from loneliness. Loneliness is a negative emotional state that we want to avoid most; it indicates deficiencies in the number or extent of one's social relationships. We may choose to spend time alone, but we don't choose to be lonely. Research suggests that adolescents spend a quarter of their time physically alone (which is more time than they spend with their families) whereas adults spend slightly more of their waking time alone, around 29 percent.[11] And we want more time alone. A *Wall Street Journal/NBC News* poll taken in the mid-1990s reported that 31 percent of US residents wanted more time to themselves, whereas only 6 percent wanted less.[12]

People want more time alone because they perceive it is as advantageous. Among the benefits linked to solitude are a sense of freedom, enhanced creativity, deepened spirituality, and ironically, a greater capacity for intimacy when one returns to the social arena. Many people experience feelings of intimacy when alone. During his stay at Walden, Thoreau wrote, "I have a great deal of company in the house, especially in the morning when nobody calls."[13] The developmental psychoanalyst Donald Winnicott contended that, as an infant, one must learn to be alone in the presence of a caregiver in order to develop the capacity to be alone as an adolescent or adult. To avoid later loneliness and anxiety, one must take the supportive environment provided by the caregiver and build it into one's view of the self and the world. I know that others love me even though I don't need constant reassurance or require their constant physical presence. I am comfortable being with myself. For this reason, Winnicott argued that the person who has developed the capacity to be alone is never truly alone.[14]

Throughout history, philosophers, spiritual leaders, and artists have attested to the benefits of solitude. Following a common template for spiritual leaders, Moses, Jesus,

Muhammad, and the Buddha all sought solitude and then returned to share with others a renewed sense of purpose and share what really matters in life. Solitude makes possible silence, allowing for communion with the divine. In solitude and silence you are drawing near to the God who "longs to be gracious to you" (Isaiah 30:18). We have the choice to connect with a power that is larger than ourselves in solitude and silence, and we can begin right now, wherever we are.

Jonathan Edwards, the great eighteenth-century New England pastor and preacher, was well known for his sojourns into nature to commune with God. In his classic psychological treatise *Religious Affections* he wrote,

> Some are greatly affected when in company, but have nothing that bears any manner of proportion to it in secret, in close meditation, prayer and conversing with God when alone, and separated from the world. A true Christian doubtless delights in religious fellowship and Christian conversation, and finds much to affect his heart in it; but he also delights at times to retire from all mankind, to converse with God in solitude. And this also has peculiar advantages for fixing his heart, and engaging his affections. True religion disposes persons to be much alone in solitary places for holy meditation and prayer . . . It is the nature of true grace, however it loves Christian society in its place, in a peculiar manner to delight in retirement, and secret converse with God.[15]

Edwards divided the affections into two groups according to whether they were characterized by approval (gratitude, love, joy) or disapproval (hatred, fear, sorrow). He believed that the approval-based affections were triggered and strengthened by time spent in solitary reflection that enabled a believer to focus inwardly in what he called the "sweet delight in God."

TRYING IT OUT

- Next time you are driving alone, resist the temptation to station surf.
- Observe yourself to see how often your own words are an attempt to fill silence.
- Try to live an entire day with no words at all (after informing your family of your goal).
- A few times a year, withdraw for a few hours to a few days to pray or meditate.
- Take a retreat at least once a year with nothing in mind but solitude. Arrange it so that you can be silent most of the time. This will take some planning, but you will find that it will recharge your gratitude batteries.

Simplicity

Tim Kasser is professor and chair of the psychology department at Knox College in Galesburg, Illinois. Tim has long studied the link between attitudes toward material goods and levels of happiness or unhappiness. Raising two boys on a farm in rural Illinois, Kasser and his wife practice what he preaches. After assuring me there was nothing inconsistent between his message and spending $30 on his book, *The High Price of Materialism*,[16] I learned that the Kassers do not have cable TV, cell phones, or the Internet at home. They watch essentially no television. They limit their sons to thirty to forty-five minutes of video games per day, though they can have more electronic time by earning coupons. They grow much of their own food. At Christmas, the boys receive stocking stuffers, one gift from Santa and one gift from their parents. In short, they live a simple and intentionally nonmaterialistic life. A materialistic lifestyle is one based on accumulation and acquisition of consumer goods beyond that which is necessary to meet basic needs.

Kasser's research demonstrates that aspiring toward greater wealth and more material possessions undermines the ability to be content. Not a terribly new idea, but Kasser advanced the argument by demonstrating that this principle applies across Western and Eastern cultures. A simple life is characterized by many different qualities, but chief among these is that it tends to be a life that eschews materialistic pursuits. A number of recent studies have found that materialism can put people in an emotional debt in that the greater they place a value on materialistic pursuits, the more at risk they are for depression and other distressing emotional states including envy and hostility. Gratitude, though, can help reduce this cost. This research documents a number of personal, societal, and environmental problems that are exacerbated by high levels of materialism. In our own research we have found that people use the pursuit and accumulation of prestige and possessions to provide them with ways to cope with feelings of insecurity and low self-esteem. Gratitude can be a corrective because it focuses on what we receive from others, and this could boost self-esteem and self-respect. Grateful people, in focusing on how others support and sustain them, view their lives as more secure and complete and are therefore less likely to turn to the accumulation of material goods to shore up an insecure self-image. An eighteen-year-old female research participant shared this with us:

> Material possessions and social status do not make a person. It is important to realize that "more" does not mean better. In fact, individuals who have more tend to take the simple things for granted because they feel entitled to certain things. Those who have less tend to appreciate what they have more. I have learned this in my life and when I look at the people around me that I used to be envious of, I realize that they have an emptiness that cannot be filled with stuff.[17]

I have no plans to lecture you on the evils of materialism or consumerism (for one thing, I am grateful that you bought this book!). I know some research psychologists mean well, but I am uncomfortable with the evangelical zeal that they display in discussing the perils of consumerism. When trying to convince people of the irreparable harm they are causing themselves, their children, and the planet when they drive to the mall to spend a leisurely Saturday afternoon in search of a replacement for a worn-out appliance or to upgrade their wardrobe, these well-meaning social scientists sometimes go beyond the data. In matters financial I lean libertarian and have no intention to impose my will on others. But as our nation endures the prolonged economic crisis that began in 2008, the findings of these studies do lend themselves to some prescriptive advice. Because gratitude involves wanting what one has rather than having what one wants, instilling a sense of gratitude may cultivate appreciation of the gifts of the moment and help you experience freedom from past regrets and future anxieties.

The Difference Between Wanting More and Wanting What You Have

In one study, Texas Tech University psychologist Jeff Larsen gave undergraduates a list of fifty-two different material items, such as a car, a stereo, or a bed, and asked them to indicate whether they possessed them. If the students owned a car, the researchers asked them to rate how much they wanted the car they had. If they didn't have a car, they were asked to rate how much they wanted one. The people who wanted more of what they had were happier than those who wanted less of what they had. However, the students who had more of what they want tended to be happier than those who had less of what they wanted. Wanting more and wanting what one already has are very different. It is not materialism per se that is the enemy of gratitude but rather a lack of appreciation for what one already possesses. Wanting things to be different than how they are right now is the formula for regret and rumination, not gratitude.

Larsen and his colleagues tested this idea by quantifying wanting and having. Participants first indicated whether or not they had an item. If they answered yes, they then answered two questions: "To what extent do you want the _____ that you have?" and "To what extent do you want a different _____?" If they answered no to the first question, they simply reported the extent to which they wanted the item.[18] Wanting more was related to more anxiety and unhappiness. It was also unrelated to wanting what one has. The take-home message is that as long as you already want what you have, wanting more does not detract from your happiness. Wanting more did not make people want what they did have any less.

Mindful Materialism

If you are reading this at home, look around you at the contents of the room you are in. Are you in the kitchen? I see my dishwasher. Am I grateful to my Bosch? Surely it does not intend to do me a favor. What about the coffeemaker? The refrigerator? Can we be grateful to our appliances?

If we subscribe to a standard conception of gratitude, then the answer must be no. My Technivorm Moccamaster coffee brewer does not intentionally provide me with a kindness every morning. But there might be another way to see it. In a blog essay entitled *Gratitude as a Measure of Technology*, Michael Sacasas suggests that there is nothing bizarre about feeling grateful for technological advances. We could in fact be grateful for material goods. I have found that if we removed entries about material things from people's gratitude journals, it would leave huge gaps. So we can think of gratitude as a measure of what lends genuine value to our lives. Sacasas poses the question of whether we could possibly measure the value of a technology by the degree to which we were grateful for it. So although I am not grateful *to* my coffeemaker I could legitimately be grateful *for* it.[19]

One way to answer this question is to ask whether you take the device for granted. We become so accustomed to the conveniences of these appliances and gadgets and devices that make our lives more pleasant that we fail to imagine what life would be like without them.

Could I do without my coffeemaker? Yes, I could boil water for tea, pick up a cup on my way to work, or even give up caffeine. But the coffeemaker is fast, convenient, quiet, and brews a darn good cup of joe. On unhurried mornings I can enjoy a steaming mug with my wife on the back patio. The caffeine jump-starts my brain so that I have a fighting chance of accomplishing something worthwhile at work, and I head to the office in a much more determined state of mind than I would have without my liquid plasma. These are experiences that add value to my day and ultimately to my life.

Thinking about gratitude and technology this way verified what I have believed for some time. We are not grateful for the object itself. Rather, we are grateful for the role the object plays within the complex dynamic of everyday experience. That is what triggers a sense of gratefulness. When it comes to happiness, material goods are not evil in and of themselves. Our ability to feel grateful is not compromised each time we leave home to go shopping or with each click of the "add-to-cart" button. When we are grateful, we can realize that happiness is not contingent on materialistic happenings in our lives but rather comes from our being embedded in caring networks of giving and receiving. Conversely, if materialism causes us to devalue our relationships, then bonds held together through the fabric of gratitude begin to unravel. Stated differently, it is not the presence of material goods that prevents us from receiving and expressing gratitude in our lives but rather what those goods might crowd out.

TRYING IT OUT

- Toss out anything that you have not used recently, say in the past six months. Any item of clothing not worn or book not opened, donate.
- Cut down on the time you spend looking for bargains or e-coupon codes. Doing so shows you are preoccupied with the price of things.
- Loan something of value to someone and do not ask for it back. If they return it, fine. If not, let it go.
- Value experiences over objects. Reflect on what recent experiences have added to your life that an object could not.
- Buy something for someone less fortunate than yourself. Spending money on others enhances gratitude and makes us happier than does spending money on ourselves. And we just might be the beneficiary of a little expressed gratitude.

Self-Reflection and Confession

People are moved to wonder by mountain peaks, by vast waves of the sea, by broad waterfall on rivers, by the all-embracing extent of the ocean, by the revolutions of the stars. But in themselves they are uninterested.

—ST. AUGUSTINE[20]

Growing up, a Saturday evening ritual in my family that I never looked forward to entailed cleansing our conscience in the confessional booth at St. Rose of Lima Catholic Church. Without confessing, we were forbidden from partaking in the Eucharist the following morning. I remember feeling like a failure if I could not come up with a mortal sin to confess. Worse, I felt I was wasting my priest's time. Confession is good for the soul, it is said. In the Christian tradition, confession is a grace and a discipline. It is a grace because it comes freely from God, but there is also an action that we must take — so it is a discipline.

The practice of self-reflection, necessary for confession, goes back many centuries and is part of most of the world's great spiritual traditions, including such diverse groups as fourth- and fifth-century Christian desert hermits and Japanese samurai.

The first-century Roman philosopher Seneca said that "we should every night call ourselves to an account; what infirmity have I mastered today? What passions opposed? What temptation resisted? What virtue acquired? Our vices will abort of themselves if they be brought every day to the shrift."[21] Although I have strayed from the Catholic roots of my childhood, I am convinced there is much to be gained from an examination of one's conscience. All spiritual traditions advocate the value of knowing thyself. Formal methods of self-reflection generally involve certain basic characteristics. First, set aside time exclusively for the purpose of self-reflection. Second, use a space, preferably with some degree of isolation, that limits external distraction. Third, apply a set of questions to help examine your life and conscience with an emphasis on your conduct in relation to other people, creatures, and objects.

In the tradition founded by St. Ignatius, the founder of the Jesuits, the examination of conscience (the Examen) is a specific method employed to assist in acquisition of one particular virtue or in the elimination of one particular vice. As such, it is very useful for anyone who wants to grow in gratitude. This prayer can be made anywhere: on the beach, in a car, at home, in the library. Many people make the Examen twice daily: once around lunchtime and again before going to bed.

There are five steps in the examination of conscience:

1. *God's presence:* No matter where you are, whether you are in front of a computer screen, in freeway traffic, mowing the lawn, in a crowd or alone, in the city or in the country, you become aware that God is present within you.
2. *Thanksgiving:* Spend a moment looking over your day with gratitude for this day's gifts. Be specific and let particular pleasures come to mind. Recall the morning dew, the smell of freshly cut grass, a strength you discovered you had. Give thanks for favors and blessings received.

3. *Self-knowledge:* Take a look at your actions, attitudes, and motives with honesty and patience. Be open to growth and learning something new about yourself.

4. *Now review your day:* Consider with a gentle look how you have responded to God's gifts. Did you receive them without grumbling or complaining? Could you have chosen gratitude rather than complaint in specific situations throughout the day?

5. *Communicate with God:* Share your thoughts on your actions, attitudes, feelings, and interactions. Perhaps during this time you may feel led to seek forgiveness, ask for direction, or share a concern, but above all give thanks for grace.

Before you start, try to be in a place where you are least likely to be disturbed and where there is the least amount of external noise. Perhaps you might light a candle or change the lighting when you pray to symbolize the start of this activity. Sit comfortably and still yourself; relax, be aware of your breathing, your body, and how you are feeling. If your first prayer is in the morning, you might resolve to avoid during the day the specific fault with which you have habitually struggled or to perform certain acts of a particular virtue in which you would like to grow. About noon you consider how often you have committed that fault or practiced that virtue and record the number so that you can keep track of your progress or decline. You then renew your resolution for the rest of the day. At night you examine and mark again and make resolutions for the following day.

Once you've done the Examen a few times, you will find your own rhythm and method. You can cover all five points daily with freedom to dwell more on one than another, as you feel moved. I have used this method with profit and find that it reliably causes my eyes to open wide in gratitude.

Ben Franklin's Moral Inventory

One of the most famous historical illustrations of moral self-examination comes from the life of Benjamin Franklin, who pursued a kind of what he called "moral perfection" by examining certain aspects of his character. When Franklin heard a Presbyterian sermon that focused on Philippians 4:8 ("Finally, brethren, whatsoever things are true, honest, just, pure, lovely, or of good report, if there be any virtue, or any praise, think on these things."), he was unsatisfied with the five virtues that the minister provided ("1. Keeping holy the Sabbath day. 2. Being diligent in reading the holy Scriptures. 3. Attending duly the publick worship. 4. Partaking of the Sacrament. 5. Paying a due respect to God's ministers."). He made his own list of thirteen virtues, divided into those related to personal behavior (temperance, order, resolution, frugality, moderation, industry, cleanliness, and tranquility) and those related to social character traits (sincerity, justice, silence, chastity, and humility). He started with one of the virtues and plotted his progress on his chart until he mastered that virtue; then he moved on to the next and continued until he tried to master them all. Determined to cure himself of moral vices, he placed each one of the virtues on a separate page in a small book that he kept with him for most of his life. He would evaluate his performance with regard to each of them every day. He would also select one of the virtues to focus on for a full week.

Was he successful? He never did master his entire list of virtues, though over time he noticed his vices diminished. One that gave him particular trouble was humility:

> In reality there is perhaps no one of our natural Passions
> so hard to subdue as Pride. Disguise it, struggle with it,
> beat it down, stifle it, mortify it as much as one pleases,
> it is still alive, and will now and then peek out and show
> itself . . . for, even if I could conceive that I had completely
> overcome it, I should probably be proud of my humility.[22]

Three Questions for Self-Reflection

The Ignatian daily Examen and Franklin's project of moral perfection are two methods for examining the self, but there are others. In working on a moral examination, you might find it effective to incorporate aspects of a Buddhist meditation technique known as *Naikan*. Naikan, developed by Yoshimoto Ishina, a self-made millionaire and devout Buddhist from Japan, is a way of helping others look inside (the word *Naikan* means "looking inside"), become introspective, and "see oneself with the mind's eye." The practice involves reflecting on three questions:

What have I received from _____?
What have I given to _____?
What troubles and difficulty have I caused _____?

A related fourth question, "What troubles and difficulties has this person caused me?" is purposely ignored in Naikan. Why? We are already experts at seeing answers to this question so we don't need any additional practice.

These three questions help us to see the reciprocal quality of our important personal relationships and provide a structure for self-reflection. We reflect on the give-and-take of our lives. Much of human life is about giving, receiving, repayment, and the gratitude that sustains this cycle. The discipline of Naikan uses our relationships with others as the mirror in which we can see ourselves and how we are sustained by the thoughts and deeds of others.

In Naikan, the first step or question can elicit feelings of gratitude when we recognize all the gifts we receive—a person's smile, kind words, or helpful actions. When we focus on the good that comes to us every day, in every situation, we can be filled with a deep thankfulness even in seemingly routine situations in our lives. For example, the next time you leave a restaurant, reflect on the number of people involved in creating a satisfying dining experience for you. Start with the valet parking attendant, move on to the person who greets and seats you, the servers who fill your water glass, bring bread, describes the daily specials, and so on. The number of people you can appreciate is staggering. And that doesn't even begin to account for the origins of all the items on the menu and the means by which they eventually wound up expertly prepared on your plate.

In the second step of Naikan, we focus on what we give to others. This helps us realize how connected we are to others and helps remove a sense of entitlement that might come from feeling that we deserve to receive without giving back. Ask yourself, In what ways might I "give back" to others as an appropriate response for the gratitude I feel? Be creative in finding ways to give back for the many blessings you have received. In the restaurant example, you can express a heartfelt thank-you to all who provided you with such a lovely experience and recommend the establishment to others.

The last step in Naikan is difficult because in it we acknowledge not the things that bother us but how we cause pain in the lives of others by our thoughts, words, and deeds. Greg Krech, who wrote on the practice of Naikan, says of this step, "If we are not willing to see and accept those events in which we have been the source of others' suffering, then we cannot truly know ourselves or the grace by which we live."[23] Recently I lost a very valuable object. I had wrongly believed that it had been deliberately taken. I stewed in feelings of anger toward the perpetrator whom I eventually discovered had found the object, placed it in a safe spot, and later went out of his way to return it to me! I started to think about times when I had caused people distress or made their life more difficult, and when I am honest I have to painfully acknowledge that I receive much more grace than I dish out.

The Naikan practice of asking these three questions can be practiced daily for twenty minutes or so in the evening to reflect on the day's activities in a general way. Or it can be used to reflect on a specific relationship over a period of fifty to sixty minutes. One can view a relationship chronologically or focus on a particular situation that might need attention. For example, if I am having a conflict with someone, I can analyze the relationship in terms of the three questions, and in so doing, discover my part in initiating or exacerbating the conflict. I come to realize what I have done and what I need to do differently. The process of Naikan emphasizes two themes: (1) the discovery of personal guilt for having been ungrateful toward people in the past and (2) the discovery of feelings of positive gratitude toward those persons who have extended themselves on your behalf in the past or present.

TRYING IT OUT

- Set aside time for personal confession and self-examination. Ask yourself, Who have I harmed by my thoughtlessness or self-centeredness? Write an apology to make things right between you and that person.
- Ask a close friend or family member to help you see your weaknesses and flaws. Be honest and try to receive his or her input with humility.
- Do a daily Naikan for one week, each day focusing on a different person in your life. Devote at least one hour a day to the three questions in the context of this relationship.
- Reflect on personal roadblocks that interfere with your ability to express gratitude in your close

relationships. Make a "what I take for granted" list in regard to that person.
- Begin with the end in mind: think about how you would like other people to remember you after you have breathed your last. Look at your life now and see if there is a gap between how you see yourself today and how you want people to remember you. Then commit to reduce this gap by practicing Naikan.

✳ PUTTING IT ALL TOGETHER ✳

In this chapter I have given you some spiritual disciplines that can serve as tools for cultivating the grateful life. This is not an exhaustive list, and feel free to implement your own spiritual disciplines in the quest for growing your gratitude. Now is the time to start putting these practices into, well, practice. Attention and intention are the ingredients to make these disciplines work. Pay attention to what you need most. Commit yourself to practicing. Banish from your mind the thought that these spiritual disciplines are limited to the saints. Nor are they limited to particular holy days or Sundays. They are for everyone, for every day.

As you commit to practicing, remember also that one size does not fit all. When it comes to creating happiness, positive psychologists have found that there is a fit between the person and happiness-inducing activities. Not all activities are equally effective for everyone. They suggest undertaking a "person-activity" fit diagnostic in which you ask yourself whether the activity feels natural, enjoyable, valuable, and if you would feel guilty if you didn't do it. You could engage in a similar self-assessment concerning each of the spiritual disciplines in this chapter. But don't be surprised if they don't always feel enjoyable or easy. The whole point of spiritual disciplines is that they counter our natural tendencies. The point is not to choose an activity because it is the easiest or most fun. The goal is to select that which you most need. Where does your weakness lie? What obstacles and roadblocks get in the way of gratitude for you? Are you perpetually overwhelmed by frantic activity? Perhaps an occasional solitude retreat will recharge you. Do you find yourself easily tempted by your surroundings? You might then consider a fast. Are you prone to taking material blessings for granted? Then simplicity might be for you.

Do not worry about what others are doing or even whether at first the exercise seems to have anything to do with gratitude. You will find that certain of these disciplines will be more effective than others. You may benefit from one exercise but not another. As you begin to reap the benefits, the progress you make will be rewarding and will increase your motivation to stay the course.

As you practice these disciplines, allow yourself a little grace. Resist the pull to be too critical of yourself. I have learned firsthand that one of the hazards in researching and writing about the virtuous life is that you constantly subject your ego to bruising. You may find yourself plagued by doubts that you are not doing these exercises well enough, consistently enough, or faithfully enough. If you allow these thoughts to hijack your consciousness, your growth in gratitude will be severely curtailed. We can work too hard to make things happen.

Instead of succumbing to this temptation, try to remember the words of the twentieth-century German theologian Paul Tillich, who said in a powerful sermon entitled *You Are Accepted* that

> sometimes at that moment a wave of light breaks into our darkness, and it is as though a voice were saying: "You are accepted. You are accepted, accepted by that which is greater than you, and the name of which you do not know. Do not ask for the name now; perhaps you will find it later. Do not try to do anything now; perhaps later you will do much. Do not seek for anything; do not perform anything; do not intend anything. Simply accept the fact that you are accepted!"[24]

This is grace and it is the basis of all gratitude.

The Biggest Obstacle to Gratitude—and Its Remedy

Since the time of the ancient philosopher Seneca or before, having an overly high opinion of oneself has been seen as the chief obstacle to feeling and expressing gratitude. Research has shown that people who are ungrateful tend to have a sense of excessive self-importance, arrogance, vanity, and a high need for admiration and approval. At the more pathological end of the scale are narcissists, people who are profoundly self-absorbed and lack the empathy needed for entering into deep, satisfying, mutually enhancing interpersonal relationships. At the more ordinary end of things are people who just feel entitled—to good grades, exemption from having to follow the rules, and special treatment of all kinds. The entitlement attitude says, "life owes me something" or "people owe me something" or "I deserve this." In all its manifestations, a preoccupation with the self can cause us to forget our benefits and our benefactors or to feel that we are owed things from others and therefore have no reason to feel thankful.

* I DESERVE THIS, SO NO THANKS *

When it comes to their children, what do you think parents say they worry about the most? The economy? Global conflict? Drugs? Moving back home after college? None of these are at the top of the list. One survey reported that two-thirds of parents said they were concerned about their children's sense

HOW ENTITLED ARE YOU?

As a quick assessment, respond to the following five statements on a seven-point scale, where 1 = strongly disagree, 2 = disagree, 3 = slightly disagree, 4 = neither disagree nor agree, 5 = slightly agree, 6 = agree, 7 = strongly agree.

_____ I honestly feel I'm just more deserving than others.
_____ Great things should come to me.
_____ If I were on the Titanic, I would deserve to be on the first lifeboat!
_____ I demand the best because I'm worth it.
_____ People like me deserve an extra break now and then.

Add up your score. If you scored twenty-five or higher, chances are that you are going to find it difficult to be grateful.[1]

of entitlement. Furthermore, when asked where this sense of entitlement comes from, 85 percent of the parents blamed themselves!

If you're like me, you probably have a whole list of things you feel entitled to, and if you don't get them, you feel cheated. If you are unable to take a vacation or buy the home you've dreamed of, then you feel life has robbed you of something you are entitled to. This is a seagull mentality. The seagulls in *Finding Nemo* flap their wings and squawk, "Mine! Mine! Mine!" and race to be the first to eat Nemo's dad, Marlin, and his friend Dory.

You know if you're into entitlement because the result leaves you constantly feeling angry, resentful, or frustrated. If you believe that someone owes you something and that person doesn't come through, you feel angry. You feel you've been ripped off and cheated out of what you believe you deserve. But entitlement is a lie. It's a perversion of reality. A sense of entitlement undermines the ability to freely accept life's blessings. There is nothing in the world that states, "Robert Emmons deserves to live a long, happy, and successful life!" My feelings of entitlement are created entirely within my own mind. For me to feel grateful for what I receive, I must translate my entitlements into gifts and recognize that I have no claim on them. If we are able to see these as given to us for our benefit without them being owed to us, we will be far less likely to develop an unhelpful attitude of entitlement.

When you feel entitled, you are not merely disappointed when others disagree with you or fail to accommodate your presumed rights, you feel cheated and wronged, and this produces anger and a stronger sense of entitlement as compensation. Resentment comes from a perception of unfairness; you're not getting the expected help, relief, consideration, praise, reward, or affection, that is, you're not getting that to which you feel entitled. You will certainly not feel grateful when you do receive what you think you have coming because, after all, you have it coming. No gift will bring grateful joy to a person who thinks they have a right to everything. Friedrich Nietzsche referred to this as *ressentiment*, the vigilant envy of others and the desire to take from them what *I* but not *they* have a right to.[2] The word *resentment* comes from the Latin word *sentire*, which means to feel, and the prefix *re* means again, so the word resent means to feel again. This means when we experience resentments, we make ourselves envious, angry, bitter, and annoyed again and again. We are weighed down in negativity, prevented from accessing gratitude and serenity. Those who are resentful are masters at rehearsing real or perceived grievances. With this their focus, they spoil each and every opportunity for current happiness.

Ingratitude is the natural offshoot of resentment. When resentful people receive a benefit, they question the motive of the giver. They wish it were more. Too little, too late, they say. Merely counting blessings will not work with this mind-set. Complaints and grumbles will always outnumber blessings and benefits. Social commentator Roger Scruton notes the following:

> Moreover, ingratitude grows in proportion to the benefits received. When those good things, like food, shelter,

education, for which our ancestors had to struggle, are offered as rights, and without cost or effort, then they are "taken for granted," as the saying is, which means quite the opposite from "taken as gifts." In such conditions there arises what we might call a culture of ingratitude—one that does not merely forget to give thanks, but regards thanks as somehow demeaning, a confession of weakness, a way of according to the other person an importance that he does not have. This thanklessness is growing around us today. It is written on the faces of pop idols and sports stars; it is announced in all kinds of ways by the media and by our political representatives. And it is one reason for the radical decline in public standards. Politicians are unlikely to behave as they should when they feel that they are acting on behalf of an entirely thankless public.[3]

Like a lone stalk of corn in a field, gratitude has no chance in this scenario. The German moral philosopher Balduin Schwarz identified the problem when he said "the ungrateful, envious, complaining man . . . cripples himself. He is focused on what he has not, particularly on that which somebody else has or seems to have, and by that he tends to poison his world."[4]

People without an attitude of entitlement tend to be satisfied with what they have and so are less susceptible to emotions such as disappointment, regret, and frustration.

✳ WHERE'S THE GRADE I PAID FOR? ✳

I have noticed an interesting shifting trend in my classes in recent years. Final exam week used to be hazardous to grandparental health. More grandparents died during finals week than in any other time of the year. Evidently they are living longer and becoming more prosperous because now they are frequently giving gifts of travel to their grandkids. Oddly enough, similar to deaths, these trips often coincide with finals week. Every quarter, I have students who are unable to take the final exam when it is scheduled because it conflicts with a vacation that their grandparents gave them. Although some understand my policy prohibiting a makeup for nonmedical reasons, others are indignant and demand that I accommodate their request to attend their family reunion on Maui.

Academic entitlement is the tendency to expect academic success without taking personal responsibility for achieving it. It is expressed in expectations of special consideration and accommodation by teachers when it comes to grades, and impatience and anger when expectations and perceived needs are not met. It is reflected in attitudes such as, "A professor should be willing to lend me his or her course notes if I ask for them," "A professor should let me arrange to turn in an assignment late if the due date interferes with my vacation plans," "I should never receive a zero on an assignment that I turned in." Diatribes about students' increasing sense of entitlement— their attitude that good grades should not be too hard to come by and that teachers should give them a "break," often accompanied by what teachers see as disrespectful and unreasonable behavior—occur frequently in faculty members' cocktail party conversations, blogs, and in opinion pieces and articles in newspapers and magazines.

The trend toward greater entitlement, general and academic, seems to be growing. In their book *The Narcissism Epidemic: Living in the Age of Entitlement* Jean Twenge and Keith Campbell report that entitlement increased by approximately 30 percent in just a fifteen-year period in children, adolescents, and young adults. It's not just entitlement that is on the rise. The average self-esteem score of college men in the mid-1990s was higher than that of 86 percent of college men in 1968, and the average self-esteem score of college women was higher than 71 percent of their peers at the earlier time point.[5]

Researchers at the University of California, Irvine, studied academic entitlement in a large and ethnically diverse group of undergraduates. They correlated scores on the academic entitlement questionnaire with perceptions of parenting and the degree to which these students feel pressure to achieve that stems from being compared to others. The findings of their study were fascinating. Among the highlights were the following:

- Asian students scored higher in entitlement than Caucasians.
- Men scored a little higher than women.
- Students high in a sense of entitlement engaged in more academic dishonesty. There was no correlation between self-esteem and academic entitlement so it does not appear that high self-esteem causes a greater sense of entitlement. In fact, the trend was for those higher in entitlement to have a slightly less positive view of themselves compared to those low in entitlement.

- Entitlement was unrelated to grade point average so the entitled students were not actually performing any better than those who felt they had to earn their grades.
- A sense of entitlement was related to more anxiety over achievement.[6]

Where does this sense of entitlement come from? It appears to be embedded to some degree in the dynamics of today's family. More academically entitled students report that their parents expect them to outperform others and reward them when they do well. They also note that their parents are always comparing them academically to siblings and to classmates, sometimes as thinly veiled curiosity ("You were in the top 5 percent. Great! I wonder who in your class scored higher?")

Although students who express stronger feelings of entitlement are more likely to cheat (e.g., copying work and turning it in as their own) in various ways, it is noteworthy that academically entitled attitudes and behaviors do not appear to pay off in higher college grades. Nor are entitled students grateful for the feedback they receive on assignments. They react to comments (especially those they perceive as unfavorable) with indignation. In my experience, the students who are grateful behave very differently and seek out more feedback. They come to my office prepared with a list of questions. These students are pleased to receive written comments, carefully reading each suggestion and seeking clarification when needed. They want extra help and are highly motivated to improve. Instead of constantly harping on how entitled our students are, we can kindle a flame of gratitude in them. Professors can help their students become more grateful and more receptive to feedback by tempering their critical feedback with praise, modeling gratitude, and sharing stories emphasizing the value and benefits of being grateful. Gratitude can also be taught to students by modeling it in the classroom. For example, when students point out something a professor overlooked or a mistake a professor made, instead of reacting defensively or becoming embarrassed, the professor could thank the students and explain that the error would not have been caught without their help. We can use a dose of humility here. This allows us to demonstrate how we all benefit when we allow our sense of self-importance to disappear and are open to correcting our mistakes. Finally, sharing stories of thankfulness about our former students or from our own lives can help our students acknowledge and identify gratitude as a positive attribute. Perhaps a story of a particularly grateful former student's success could be shared to help make the benefits of gratitude and optimism more obvious and tangible to students. I keep a file of all the letters and e-mails I have received from former students in which they have expressed some gratitude toward me. Professors could also share their own personal experiences, possibly detailing their gratitude to another professor for all of the helpful feedback they received when working on scholarship or on teaching. These stories provide students with examples of how being appreciative of help has benefited others and could suggest to them that gratefulness might benefit them as well.

Sally: This place is a disaster! Why didn't you load the
dishwasher, fold the towels, and take out the overflowing
recycling?

Harry: I didn't notice.

Exchanges of this type take place daily in homes across
the country. Sally wonders how Harry could not have seen
what needs to be done, whereas Harry claims earnestly that he
really didn't notice the mess and didn't understand why Sally
is so upset. To make matters worse, not only does their unaware
partner fail to notice what needs to be done, they don't even
notice when their partner takes care of these problems. This
isn't just about division of labor but about the expression of
gratitude that's important to a strong and lasting relationship.

In the 1980s, University of California, Berkeley, sociologist
Arlie Hochschild identified a source of tension in marriages that
she called "the economy of gratitude,"[7] which explains why
underperformers such as Harry often aren't grateful for their
partner's efforts and don't pitch in their fair share. Hochschild
argues that, in relationships, individuals offer each other "gifts,"
which are something extra, beyond what is expected. Therefore,
if the laundry (or trash, or dishes, or all of the above) is defined
as "yours," then your partner is unlikely to feel gratitude toward
you for doing it. After all, you are just doing what you are supposed to do, what you are so much better at doing. In fact,
because the undone task bothers you more than the other

person, maybe you are really only doing it for yourself. Thus, he is unlikely to feel gratitude—because he doesn't view your efforts as a gift to him. Interestingly, this theory is originally based on studies of social networks and division of labor among ants and bees. In her research, entomologist Jennifer Fewell found that certain bees were almost always the ones to take action once the level of honey in the hive had dropped to a particular level. In addition, she discovered that their work reduced the chance that other, underperforming bees would do the job in the future.[8]

Researchers at Arizona State University suggest one of the keys to determining who will perform a specific household task is each partner's "response threshold," which describes the degree of disorder that must exist before someone is sufficiently bothered to perform a task that's not being done. Individuals with low response thresholds for a specific task are moved to perform the task earlier than those who have a higher threshold. In terms of the division of labor, then, household partners often develop this pattern: the person with the lower threshold performs tasks before the partner is moved to do so, the tasks come to be defined as "hers," the partner does not feel responsible for performing the task—and he does not feel grateful, because the overperformer is just doing "her" job . . . all of which makes him less likely to lend a hand in the future. One couple's conflict centered on this issue:

> She (the wife) complained about how unappreciative he (her husband) was of the effort she took in making gourmet dinners and keeping the house clean. He said, "Hang on a

minute. I never asked her to do anything of those things. I can't help it if she has higher standards than I do. I don't *care* what we have for dinner. I don't *care* if the floor gets mopped twice a week."[9]

More important, gratitude can help alter the dynamics of couples' division of labor. Expressing gratitude reminds the less-involved partner that the division of labor is not fair and that his partner's contributions are a gift. And because people who receive gifts typically feel obligated to reciprocate, this insight can lead the less-involved partner to offer "gifts" of his own by contributing more to household tasks. In addition, the overper-forming partner is likely to experience less resentment and frustration once her efforts are recognized and appreciated.

For a number of years my wife and I have had a schedule in which I come home at noon on Fridays and perform the household duties that she takes care of on the other four and one-half weekdays. At the very least, this opportunity gives me a much deeper appreciation of what is entailed in running a household when I am comfortably settled in front of my computer in my campus office. It is a good reminder not to take for granted what I might otherwise do.

The economy of gratitude, then, helps to explain the fact that husbands and wives are most satisfied in their marriages when one views a partner's household labor as a gift, over and above what is expected. Researchers have found that individuals who feel appreciated by their partners do indeed express less resentment over the division of labor and greater satisfaction with their relationships than do those who feel that they are taken for granted.

* HUMILITY AND GRATITUDE *

After an unsuccessful battle with alcoholism, Bill Wilson had a profound religious conversion experience that caused him to reorder his priorities and opened the doorway to abstinence. He then used his life lessons to promote a twelve-step approach to the treatment of alcoholism that we now know as Alcoholics Anonymous. Humility-related themes played a central role within Wilson's twelve-step framework (e.g., admitting personal and moral limitations, making amends, relying on a higher power). Yet throughout his life Bill often wavered between low self-esteem and arrogance, struggling to come to terms with his own personal demons while managing near-celebrity status in what was supposed to be an anonymous self-help organization. Bill Wilson was clearly someone who understood the central value of humility. However, he also understood firsthand the difficulty of attaining it consistently, and he wrestled through-out his lifetime in his attempts to cultivate it. Wilson was hardly alone in his quest.[10] The poet T. S. Eliot said that humility was one of the most difficult virtues to achieve because we all desire to think well of ourselves.

What is humility? Although the etymological roots of humility are in lowliness and self-abasement (from the Latin term *humilis* meaning "lowly, humble," or literally "on the ground" and from the Latin term *humus* meaning "earth"), the emerging consensus among science and religion scholars is that humility is a psychological and intellectual virtue or a character strength. Those who are humble have the following:

- A clear and accurate (not underestimated) sense of their abilities and achievements
- The ability to acknowledge their mistakes, imperfections, gaps in knowledge, and limitations (often with reference to a God or to a higher power)
- An openness to new ideas, contradictory information, and advice
- The ability to keep their abilities and accomplishments in perspective
- Relatively low levels of self-absorption and an ability to forget the self
- An appreciation of the value of all things as well as the many different ways that people and things can contribute to our world

Another definition of humility, based in modern Jewish thought, is helpful for understanding why it is needed for gratitude. In this view, humility is limiting oneself to an appropriate space while leaving room for others. Rabbi Rafael, a nineteenth-century Hassidic teacher told a story that depicts the perils of thinking too highly of oneself:

When I get to heaven, they'll ask me, why didn't you learn more Torah? I will tell them I was not bright enough. Then they'll ask me, why didn't you do more kind deeds for others? I will tell them that I was physically weak. Then they'll ask me, why didn't you give more to charity? And I'll tell them that I didn't have enough money for that. And then they'll ask me, If you were so stupid, weak and poor, why were you so arrogant? And for that I won't have an answer.[11]

In contemporary society, it is easy to overlook the merits of humility. Some might think of a humble person as a weak and passive sort, someone who keeps eyes downcast and deflects all praise and is completely lacking in self-respect and confidence. Others associate humility with humiliation, prompting images of shame, embarrassment, or self-disgust. In politics, business, and sports, the egoists command our attention. "Show me some-one without an ego," said real estate mogul Donald Trump, "and I'll show you a loser." At the opposite end of the spectrum was the philosopher Spinoza, who said that "humility brings more advantages than disadvantages."

Modern scientific research supports Spinoza more so than Trump. Studies reveal that the unassuming virtue of humility, rather than representing weakness or inferiority, as is com-monly assumed, is a strength of character that produces posi-tive, beneficial results for self and society. Humility is one of the most expansive and life-enhancing of all the virtues, out of fashion though it may be. Humble people are more likely to flourish in life, in more domains, than are people who are less humble. Consider a handful of findings from recent research studies and surveys:

- People who say they feel humble when they are praised report that the experience made them want to be nice to people, increase their efforts, and challenge themselves.
- Humble people are more admired and the trait of humility is viewed positively by most.
- Humble teachers are rated as more effective and humble lawyers as more likeable by jurors.
- CEOs who possess a rare combination of extreme humility and strong professional will were catalysts for transforming a good company into a great one.
- More than 80 percent of adults surveyed indicated that it is important that professionals demonstrate modesty and humility in their work (though not necessarily about themselves).
- Humility is positively associated with academic success in the form of higher grades.
- Humility is a quality of moral exemplars, people who dedicate their lives to noble purposes. Millard Fuller, founder of Habitat for Humanity International, spent his life pursuing the vision of giving people homes all around the world and in his talks and writings spoke honestly as much about his failures as his successes.[12]

Do you think you are you a humble person? For obvious reasons, you cannot rate your own level of humility. It's an elusive concept to get at scientifically. "I am very humble" is self-contradictory. This has not discouraged personality psychologists from developing questionnaires to measure it, albeit indirectly. For example, to what extent do you identify with each of the following statements:

I generally have a good idea about the things I do well or do poorly.

I have difficulty accepting advice from other people.

I try my best in things but I realize that I have a lot of work to do in many areas.

I am keenly aware of how little I know about the world.

Questions such as these tap various facets of the humble personality, including an appreciation and recognition of one's limitation and an accurate assessment of oneself. People who score high on this questionnaire also tend to score high on our gratitude questionnaire because humility goes hand-in-hand with gratitude. The most grateful people I know are also the most humble people. Mark T. Mitchell, professor of political science at Patrick Henry College in Virginia, writes, "Gratitude is born of humility, for it acknowledges the giftedness of the creation and the benevolence of the Creator. This recognition gives birth to acts marked by attention and responsibility. Ingratitude, on the other hand, is marked by hubris, which denies the gift, and this always leads to inattention, irresponsibility, and abuse."[13] Studies have shown that humble people feel better about receiving help from others. Unlike the proud, they do not mind admitting they need assistance.

We Did Not Create Ourselves

Humility is a key to gratitude because living humbly is the truest approach to life. Returning to the etymological origins of humility, humble people are grounded in the truth that they need others. We all need help from others. We are not self-sufficient. We did not will ourselves into being. The well-known moral philosopher Alasdair MacIntyre said that we are all "dependent rational animals."[14] We are born as beings dependent on others for survival, and most of us end life dependent on others as well. We have a few good decades in between where we are proud of our independence but we never fully achieve it because the nature of human life requires us to be interdependent. We are continually faced with the temptation to deny this fundamental reality but it is unavoidable. We depend on parents, friends, our pets, the government, God, the Earth, and other providers of the goods of our lives. Seeing with grateful eyes requires that we see the web of interconnection in which we alternate between being givers and receivers. In *The Sacred Depths of Nature*, cell biologist Ursula Goodenough writes,

> We are called to acknowledge our dependency on the web of life both for our subsistence and for countless aesthetic experiences: spring birdsong, swelling treebuds, the dizzy smell of honeysuckle. We are called to acknowledge that which we are not: we cannot survive in a deep-sea vent, or fix nitrogen, or create a forest canopy, or soar 300 feet in the air and then catch a mouse in a spectacular nosedive.[15]

At a conference a few years ago, I made the comment that it is impossible to be grateful to oneself. I thought this would be uncontroversial. To my surprise, I was challenged by a graduate student who claimed that not only was it possible to be grateful to oneself but that he himself had experienced this feeling many times. He proceeded to shadow me for the rest of the conference, trying to come up with some convincing examples of self-directed gratitude. I was not persuaded to change my position. We can be proud of a personal accomplishment or satisfied that we have achieved a sought-after goal. We can take credit for good decisions and be pleased by our own performance, but there is no place for gratitude here. We can give ourselves gifts, but I doubt that would result in a feeling of thankfulness. There is no surge of thankfulness when we unwrap a gift that we've given ourselves; there is no desire to give back generously out of gratitude to ourselves. This is why we cannot be grateful to ourselves. The logic of gratitude requires a giver, a gift, and a receiver; a benefactor, a beneficiary, and a benefit. That is why gratitude is always directed outward. It is a relational feeling that requires the presence of another. It is a response that is channeled to go outside the self.

Cultivating Humility

If humility is the antidote to entitlement and a lack of gratitude, how can we get more of it? It is almost a contradiction to try to be humble. If we set humility as a personal goal and then succeed at it, would we not be proud of our accomplishment and thus not humble? As Ted Turner once remarked, "If I only had a little humility, I would be perfect."[16] Humility appears to be so little, so meek, so unassuming, so well, humble. But we should not be deceived. The more I contemplate the requirements for cultivating gratitude, the more I am convinced of the necessity of humility. In gratitude and humility we turn to realities outside of ourselves. We become aware of our limitations and our need to rely on others. In gratitude and humility, we acknowledge the myth of self-sufficiency. We look upward and outward to the sources that sustain us. Becoming aware of realities greater than ourselves shields us from the illusion of being self-made, being here on this planet by right—expecting everything and owing nothing. The humble person says that life is a gift to be grateful for, not a right to be claimed. Humility ushers in a grateful response to life.

Paul Wong, president of the International Network on Personal Meaning, provides a set of twenty humble practices for daily life:

- Acknowledging our wrongdoing
- Receiving correction and feedback graciously
- Refraining from criticizing others
- Forgiving others who have wronged us
- Apologizing to others we have wronged
- Enduring unfair treatments with patience and a forgiving spirit
- Thinking and speaking about the good things of other people
- Rejoicing over other people's success
- Counting our blessings for everything, good and bad

- Seeking opportunities to serve others
- Being willing to remain anonymous in helping others
- Showing gratitude for our successes
- Giving due credit to others for our successes
- Treating success as a responsibility to do more for others
- Being willing to learn from our failures
- Assuming responsibility for our failures
- Accepting our limitations and circumstances
- Accepting the social reality of discrimination and prejudice
- Treating all people with respect regardless of their social status
- Enjoying the lowly status of being an outsider and a nobody[17]

You will see gratitude sprinkled throughout this list as well as a focus on the concerns of others and a sense of acceptance of self and others. In humility there is a lack of defensiveness regarding one's own self-worth. With so little need to defend the self, the humble person has more energy to invest in the lives of others. Humble people do not deny their talents but rather keep a proper perspective. They not need to denigrate others to feel better about themselves. Others do not have to lose so they can win.

Why did Wong suggest so many practices? Because humility is one of the most difficult virtues to cultivate. It does not come easily or naturally, particularly in a culture that values self-aggrandizement. This list is a great beginning, and every one of these twenty practices will cultivate humility. But I know what you are thinking: twenty is way too many. Let me suggest instead three very good practices for developing humility that can help us see through more grateful eyes. Try out each one of these by writing in your journal about it. Devote some time to them. They just might change the way you think about humility.

What Are Your Perceptions of Humility?

One way to raise your humility consciousness and therefore take the first step toward developing more humility is to define it. Do you think humility is the same as low self-esteem or modesty, humiliation, or shame? To what extent do you think it would be good if you were more humble? To what extent do you think it would be bad if you were less humble? Recall a real-life situation in which you felt humble. Briefly describe the situation, why you felt humble in that situation, and what emotions you experienced when you felt humble. Did the feeling of humility help or hinder what you were trying to accomplish in the situation? Why can it be so difficult to live humbly? Are there personal or cultural forces that undermine humility? These questions can lead to a rich examination and discussion of the nature and benefits of humility within your own life and inspire you to consider ways in which humility might be encouraged in your relationships with others.

Who Are the Most Humble People You Know?

Think about the most humble person you know. This may be someone with whom you are in a relationship or someone whom you have never met. One of my own personal heroes of humility is the twentieth-century British writer G. K. Chesterton.

Hailed as one of the most influential writers of his age, Chesterton's humility is legendary. Chesterton understood that the key to happiness and gratitude is humility. It is said that the *Times* once invited readers to answer the question, "What's wrong with the world?" Chesterton's response was the shortest of those submitted—he simply wrote, "Dear Sirs, I am. Sincerely yours, G. K. Chesterton."[18]

After identifying an exemplar, think about why he or she is seen as humble, other qualities likely to be found in this person, and situations in which his or her humility was revealed. Spend fifteen minutes writing about how the person you picked illustrates various aspects of humility. In what ways would you want to be more like him or her? Do you think that the person actively tries to be humble or is it just a fundamental way of being for him or her? How can you become more like this exemplar?

How Can Contemplation Cultivate Humility?

Imagine experiencing this state: You feel a deep sense of peace and internal balance—you are at harmony with yourself, with others, and with your larger environment. You experience increased buoyancy and vitality. Your senses are enlivened—every aspect of your perceptual experience seems richer, more textured. Surprisingly, you feel invigorated even when you would usually have felt tired and drained. Things that usually would irk you just don't get to you as much. Your body feels regenerated—your mind clear. At least for a period of time, decisions become obvious as priorities clarify and inner conflict dissolves. Intuitive insight suddenly provides convenient solutions to problems that had previously consumed weeks of restless thought. Your creativity flows freely. You may experience a sense of greater connectedness with others and feelings of deep fulfillment.[19]

Most people have at some point in their lives experienced a state similar to that just described. Whether these magical moments are called peak experiences, states of flow, or spiritual epiphanies, these self-transcendent states not only expand the self but also, paradoxically, result in a feeling of humility in the presence of something larger and grander than the self. However, awe-inspiring experiences could certainly provide one route for increasing humility. When undergraduates in one study were asked to identify situations in which they felt humble, a number of them identified those involving contemplation of natural wonders.

Consistent with the positive outcomes produced by humility, these moments when the self is transcended drive optimal functioning across nearly all spheres of human experience, including cognitive flexibility, creativity, and innovative problem solving. They promote helpfulness, generosity, and effective cooperation.

Eliminating entitlement from your life and embracing gratitude and humility are spiritually and psychologically liberating. Gratitude is the recognition that life owes me nothing and all the good I have is a gift. It is a response to all that has been given. It is not a getting of what we may desire. My eyes are a gift. So is my wife, my clothes, my job, and my every breath. This is a major shift. Recognizing that everything good in life is ultimately a gift is a fundamental truth of reality. Humility makes that recognition possible. The humble person says, "How can I not be filled with overflowing gratitude?"

A powerful, although tragic, example of someone who grasped the gratitude attitude was a Jewish woman named Bruria. The story of Bruria is told in the Talmud, a central text in the Jewish faith. Bruria and her husband, Rabbi Meir, had two sons who both died one Friday afternoon before Shabbat. Bruria decided not to tell her husband of the tragedy until after Shabbat because, according to Jewish law, one is not permitted to have a funeral on Shabbat or to openly mourn. There was nothing they could do until after Shabbat so she kept the information to herself and allowed her husband to enjoy the day (imagine being able to do that!). Explaining where the boys were was the least of her challenges. When Shabbat was over Bruria broke the horrible news to her husband. She asked him a legal question: what is the proper course of action if one person borrows two jewels from another and then the original owner requests the return of the jewels? He replied with the obvious answer that one is obligated to return the loan on demand. She then took her husband to where their two dead sons lay and said, "God has requested that we return the loan of our two jewels."[20] Bruria teaches us a potentially life-transforming lesson here: everything we have is on loan.

Gratitude, Suffering, and Redemption

L ife is suffering." So begins one of the best-selling psychology books of all times.[1] The conclusion that suffering is endemic to the human condition derives from centuries of philosophical, theological, and psychological literatures all around the world. To live is to face the inevitability of loss: death of a spouse, family member, or friend; loss of health; terminal illness; birth of a child with a physical or mental challenge; divorce; job loss; end of a love relationship; loss of a beloved pet—the list goes on and on. One of the basic truths that forms the cornerstone of virtually all of the world's great wisdom traditions is that *life is suffering*. For example, the first of the Four Noble Truths of Gautama Buddha is that life inevitably involves *dukhha* (suffering). The Buddha acknowledged that there is happiness and sorrow in the world, but he taught that even when we have some kind of happiness, it is not permanent; it is subject to change. In Hinduism, mental and physical suffering is thought to be part of the unfolding of karma and is the consequence of inappropriate action (mental, verbal, or physical) that occurred in either one's current life or in a past life. It is not seen as punishment but as a natural consequence of the moral laws of the universe operating in response to past negative behavior. To view suffering as bad is to see only one side of it. Suffering can be positive if it leads to progress on a spiritual path or an awakened sense of gratitude for the positive aspects of life. Some even embrace suffering as a way to progress, a way to be tested and learn from a difficult experience.

The lessons that religion teach is that suffering can be transformed and difficult experiences can be reversed or redeemed. The possibility that life's adversities may serve as a catalyst for personal growth is a familiar theme in psychological writings as well. In his study of self-actualizers, Abraham Maslow noted that "the most important learning experiences . . . were tragedies, deaths, and trauma . . . which forced change in the life-outlook of the person and consequently in everything that he did."[2] The ability to perceive the elements (negative and positive) in one's life and even life itself as gifts would appear essential if we are to transform tragedies into opportunities. Cultivating this level of gratitude allows us to heal from past wounds and look forward to the future with a fresh affirmation toward life. We realize that we can *be* grateful even if we don't *feel* grateful. Suffering can be a reason for gratefulness in that it shatters our illusions of self-sufficiency, causes us to be accountable, and teaches us what is truly important.

Experiences of loss and disappointment can remove the superficial things in our lives that we cling to for meaning, allowing us to see things of value that we had never before noticed. Recent years have seen an explosive increase in research on stress-related growth and trauma-induced transformation. Unexpected capacities emerge, existing relationships once taken for granted become more precious, awareness and insight into what really matters in life is realized, spiritual senses are heightened.

Don't get me wrong. I am not suggesting that this will come easily or naturally. It's not going to be easy to be grateful for the hard stuff. No one "feels" grateful that he or she has lost a job or a home or good health or has taken a devastating hit on his or her retirement portfolio. For example, a mother wrote this to me in an e-mail:

> I lost my beloved son to melanoma a year ago and both my daughter-in-law and myself are struggling to maintain our emotions. We both have fallen into a deep depression and haven't been able to recover. I know it takes time for our hearts to heal and focus on being grateful for all the years we had together. My son was only 38 years old and was in the prime of his life. I am angry that he was taken from me and I am angry that the medical field misdiagnosed him for over 9 months and then it was too advanced . . . it's just very hard to be happy any longer.[3]

Are we going to tell her to cheer up and focus on what she still has to be grateful for? No. She knew in her head that gratitude was the best approach to take but even a year after losing her son she was not ready to reach that stage. But it is nevertheless possible for her to get to that point eventually if she is able to cultivate gratitude as a way of being.

In the aftermath of the economic maelstrom that has gripped our country, I have often been asked if people are able to summon the courage to feel grateful under such dire circumstances. My response is that not only will a grateful attitude help but it is also *essential*. In fact, it is precisely under crisis conditions when we have the most to gain by a grateful perspective on life. In the face of demoralization, gratitude has the power to energize. In the face of brokenness, gratitude has the power to heal. In the face of despair, gratitude has the power to bring hope.

I believe that gratitude is the best approach to life. When life is going well, it allows us to celebrate and magnify the goodness. When life is going badly, it provides a perspective by which we can view life in its entirety and not be overwhelmed by temporary circumstances. And this is what grateful people do. They have learned to transform adversity into opportunity no matter what happens, to see existence itself as a gift. Seeing life in this way requires that gratefulness be a deep and abiding aspect of a person's character, developed patiently using the practices we've been discussing in this book.

It is vital to make a distinction between *feeling* grateful and *being* grateful. We don't have much control over our emotions. We cannot easily will ourselves to feel grateful, to feel less depressed, or to feel happy. Feelings follow from the way we look at the world, thoughts we have about the way things are, the way things should be, and the distance between these two points. But being grateful is a choice, a prevailing attitude that endures and is relatively immune to the gains and losses that flow in and out of our lives. I also don't want to imply that the attitude of gratitude can be learned easily in the context of hard times. Sometimes we have to start slow. The Grammy award–winning singer-songwriter Mary Chapin Carpenter describes her own learning curve of gratitude. About to embark on an upcoming tour, she suffered a pulmonary embolism (blood clot in her lung), which nearly proved fatal. During her recuperation, she was beset with feelings of anxiety, pain, fear, and depression. What seemed a casual comment—by a grocery store clerk asking her how she was—turned her mind to the simple appreciation of the giftedness of that day, the next day, and to days beyond that one. She wrote,

> I don't know if my doctors will ever be able to give me the precise reason why I had a life-threatening illness. I do know that the young man in the grocery store reminded me that every day is all there is, and that is my belief . . . The learning curve of gratitude, however, is showing me exactly how human I am.[4]

Cultivating an attitude of gratitude before loss or tragedy strikes builds up a sort of psychological immune system that can cushion us when we fall. There is scientific evidence that grateful people are more resilient to stress in general and at all levels, whether minor everyday hassles or major personal upheavals. Furthermore, trials and suffering can actually refine and deepen gratefulness if we allow them to show us not to take things for granted. Our national holiday of gratitude, Thanksgiving, has a history of growing during hard times. The first Thanksgiving was after nearly half the pilgrims died following a rough winter and year. It became a national holiday in 1863 in the middle of the Civil War and was moved to its current date in the 1930s following the Depression. Is there any significance to the growth of this holiday? Are we better off counting our blessings in harder times than in good times?

* BAD TO GOOD *

In October 1929 the stock market crashed and people throughout this nation began to feel the effects of what was to become known as the Great Depression. Life savings were wiped out and jobs and incomes that were taken for granted dried up overnight. Bread lines formed in the streets of cities across the country. One of the darkest times in this nation's history was on us.

In mid-November of that year, a group of church leaders came together in Boston to determine what message they could give to their flock at the upcoming Thanksgiving services. Some wanted to skip the topic altogether, thinking that it would not be appropriate to ask people to focus on gratitude in the midst of their suffering. However, Pastor William Stiger rallied the troops and told them this was not the time avoid the topic of thanksgiving; this is exactly what people needed to hear at this time. In times like this, he told them, we need to be most thankful and most need to affirm the goodness that remains despite current afflictions.

This is just one illustration in a long historical tradition of the juxtaposition of suffering with thanksgiving. Gratitude starts with remembering and memory of adversity serves as a basis for thanksgiving. In his book *The Good Life*, the late Reverend Peter Gomes of Harvard University cites the nineteenth-century pilgrim Baptists whose theme of the first service in their new sanctuary following years of adversity was "our years of affliction serve to enhance our present joy."[5] In ancient near-Eastern culture, the Israelites celebrated deliverance from oppression and slavery with public proclamations of God's faithfulness as written about in the Hebrew scriptures. In these stories, affliction or suffering are redeemed by the recognition of goodness received, accompanied by powerful feelings of contrast and relief. When times are good, people take prosperity for granted and begin to believe that they are invulnerable. In times of uncertainty, people realize how powerless they are to control their own destiny and this realization can lead to the perception of a deeper reality. If you begin to see that everything you have, everything you have counted on, everything that you think matters to your well-being may be taken away, gratitude becomes a way of rebuilding one's foundation so that it can never be demolished.

The contrast between suffering and redemption serves as the basis for one of my tips for practicing gratitude: remember the bad. Bad to good contrast thinking works this way: think of the worst times in your life, your sorrows, your losses, your sadness and then remember that here you are, able to remember them, that you made it through the worst times of your life, you got through the trauma, you got through the trial, you endured the temptation, you survived the bad relationship, you're making your way out of the dark. Remember the bad things, then look to see where you are now. This process of remembering how difficult life used to be and how far we have come sets up an explicit contrast in our minds that is fertile ground for gratefulness. Our minds think in terms of counterfactuals—mental comparisons we make between the way things are and how things might have been different or are now different from how things were.

Contrasting the present with negative times in the past can make us feel happier (or at least less *un*happy) and enhance our overall sense of well-being. Emotion researcher Nico Frijda proposed two laws of emotion that can help explain why such redemptive shifts result in gratitude.[6] First, the law of change states that our feelings are elicited not by events themselves but by actual or expected changes in those events. If I am expecting a quiet, relaxing evening at home with my wife and arrive home and learn that our dog has run away, our in-laws are visiting, and the toilets are backed up, that causes a severe shift in my feelings as I realize how far reality is from my expectations. If, however, I arrive expecting the worst and my wife has prepared for me a romantic candlelight dinner and the kids and the dog are snuggled in their beds, my gratitude will be immeasurable. The greater the change from expectations, the more intense is the emotional reaction. This accounts for why we suffer so much when we lose something we have taken for granted, be it our health, satisfying work, or a cherished relationship. A degree of uncertainty or surprise, as I discussed in chapter 2, contributes to the magnitude of the feeling. Losing something and getting it back is another example that may be familiar to you. Consider the joy of the father in the parable of the prodigal son told in the New Testament: "For this son of mine was dead and is alive again; he was lost and is found" as he hugged the son on his return and arranged for a huge welcome home celebration.

Nico Frijda's second law of emotion concerns comparative feeling: the intensity of emotion depends on the relationship between an event and some frame of reference against which the event is evaluated. We are constantly comparing our current state with what we have experienced in the past or what we desire to have happen, what we see happening to other people, and so on. There are many potential frames of reference. For example, I see people around me struggling financially and I feel content even though I have not had a pay raise in years.

Try this little exercise to see how your gratitude today can benefit from a contrast perspective from a past event. First, think about one of the unhappiest events you have experienced. How often do you find yourself thinking about this event today? Does the contrast with the present make you feel grateful and pleased? Do you realize your current life situation is not as bad as it could be? Try to realize and appreciate just how much better your life is now. Does this help you see that you have little reason to complain about anything in the present? The point is not to ignore or forget the past but to develop a fruitful current frame of reference from which to view experiences and events.

A further illustration of the "bad to good" phenomenon comes from research on confronting one's own mortality. This recent study found that thinking about one's own death could make a person more grateful for the life that he or she has.[7] Researchers asked participants to imagine a "death" scenario (do not try out this idea at a dinner party) where, trapped in a high rise, they are overcome by smoke and perish in a fire. They were then asked to respond to a series of questions convening their present levels of gratitude. The death reflection condition produced a greater increase in gratitude in comparison to two control conditions. Confronting the possibility of dying may lead a person to realize the accuracy of the British writer G. K. Chesterton's insight that "life is not only a pleasure but a kind of eccentric privilege."[8]

∗ COPING GRATEFULLY ∗

As the German theologian and Lutheran pastor Dietrich Bonhoeffer once said, "Gratitude changes the pangs of memory into a tranquil joy."[9] We know that gratitude enhances happiness, but why? Gratitude maximizes happiness in multiple ways, and one reason why gratitude works is that it helps us reframe memories of unpleasant events in such a way that it decreases their unpleasant emotional impact. This implies that grateful coping entails looking for positive consequences of negative events. For example, grateful coping might involve seeing how a stressful event has shaped who we are today and has prompted us to reevaluate what is really important in life.

To imply that gratitude is a helpful strategy to handle hurt feelings does not mean that suffering and pain are ignored or denied. The field of positive psychology has at times been criticized for its perceived failure to acknowledge the value of negative emotions. Barbara Held of Bowdoin College in Maine, for example, contends that positive psychology has been too negative about negativity and too positive about positivity. To deny that life has its share of disappointments, frustrations, losses, hurts, setbacks, and sadness would be unrealistic and untenable given the realities of life. Life *is* suffering. No amount of positive-thinking exercises will change this truth. If people feel bad about life's many difficulties and they cannot manage to transcend their pain no matter how hard they try (to feel grateful), they could end up feeling even worse; they could feel guilty or defective for not having the right attitude, in addition to whatever was ailing them in the first place.[10] She is not alone in these sentiments. In her book *Healing Through the Dark Emotions* therapist Miriam Greenspan has this to say about unpleasant feelings:

> We pay psychotherapists to cure it, take Prozac to mute it,
> seek counsel from religions that exhort us to rise above
> it, read inspirational books to overcome it, join recovery
> programs and self-help groups to cope with it, spend
> millions to escape it, use alcohol, drugs, food, work,

possessions, sex, entertainment, and all the techno-toys we can get to distract ourselves from it.[11]

These points are well taken, and certainly much harm can be done by telling people to simply buck up, count their blessings, and remember how much they still have to be grateful for. Processing a life experience through a grateful lens does not mean denying negativity. It is not a form of superficial happiology. It *does* mean realizing the power you have to transform an obstacle into an opportunity. It means reframing a loss into a potential gain, recasting negativity into positive channels for gratitude. A growing body of research has examined how grateful recasting works.

In a study conducted at Eastern Washington University, participants were randomly assigned to one of three writing groups that would recall and report on an unpleasant open memory (about some typically emotionally charged or unpleasant unfinished business from their past—a loss, a betrayal, victimization, or some other personally upsetting experience). All participants wrote for twenty minutes on three sessions about one of three topics: (1) issues that were irrelevant to their open memory, (2) their experience pertaining to their open memory, and (3) the positive consequences of the open memory event that they can now feel grateful about. Instructions for the third group were as follows:

> Please recall your open memory that you remembered for this study. For the next 20 minutes we would like you to write about your open memory. Think again about this experience

for a few moments. At first it may seem that the event you wrote down might not have had any positive effects upon your life. However, sometimes even when bad things happen, they ultimately have positive consequences, things we can now be grateful for. Try to focus on the positive aspects or consequences of this difficult experience. As the result of this event, what kinds of things do you now feel thankful or grateful for? How has this event benefited you as a person? How have you grown? Were there personal strengths that grew out of your experience? How has the event made you better able to meet the challenges of the future? How has the event put your life into perspective? How has this event helped you appreciate the truly important people and things in your life? In sum, how can you be thankful for the beneficial consequences that have resulted from this event? As you write, do not worry about punctuation or grammar, just really let go and write as much as you can about the positive aspects of your experience that you feel you now can be grateful for.[12]

The most common type of open memory concerned romantic rejection, not too surprising given these were undergraduates. Results showed that grateful writing was highly effective. Participants who looked for gratitude in the experience showed more closure and less unpleasant emotional impact than participants who just wrote about the experience without being prompted to see ways it might be redeemed. Participants were never told not to think about the negative aspects of the experience or to deny or ignore the pain. Moreover, participants who found reasons to be grateful demonstrated fewer intrusive memories, such as wondering why it happened, whether it could have been prevented, or if they believed they caused it to happen. Thinking gratefully, this study showed, can promote healing of troubling memories and in a sense redeem them. Other studies have shown that you do not have to write for twenty minutes. Laura King at the University of Missouri found evidence for what she called a "two-minute miracle." Just a couple of minutes of writing about good events in one's life may be enough to produce positive emotional effects.[13]

Anjali Mishra, a graduate student in my laboratory at the University of California, Davis, continued this line of research about writing gratefully about past hurts. She asked students to write about a personally upsetting event from one of three perspectives. One group wrote about the event from a gratitude perspective and the others wrote about it factually or focused solely on their feelings about the event. The general instructions were as follows:

> Think about and focus on a significant personal life experi-
> ence that was highly upsetting in nature. This experience
> may have been associated with feelings of loss, rejection,
> anger, sadness, anxiety, or frustration. Try to choose an
> experience that you think about often and that still hasn't
> been totally resolved in your mind. Think about the
> experience for a few moments . . . even negative life events
> can ultimately have positive consequences leading to feelings
> of gratitude. For the next 20 minutes describe and write in
> detail how you have grown as a person and any feelings of
> thankfulness that you felt since the traumatic event.[14]

These stories are tough to read. Parental divorce, romantic betrayals, alcohol abuse, loss of a pet, academic failures, sexual assault, horror story after horror story. Results revealed that writing gratefully increased students' ability to find some meaning in the event. Those in the gratitude writing condition were more likely to say that they had been able to make some sense of the experience and had more hope for the future compared to participants in the other two experimental conditions.

If you are troubled by an open memory or a past unpleasant experience, you might consider trying to reframe how you think about it using the language of thankfulness. The unpleasant experiences in our lives don't have to be of the traumatic variety in order for us to gratefully benefit from them. Whether it is a large or small event, here are some additional questions to ask yourself:

- What lessons did the experience teach me?
- Can I find ways to be thankful for what happened to me now even though I was not at the time it happened?
- What ability did the experience draw out of me that surprised me?
- How am I now more the person I want to be because of it?
- Have my negative feelings about the experience limited or prevented my ability to feel gratitude in the time since it occurred?
- Has the experience removed a personal obstacle that previously prevented me from feeling grateful?

A twenty-three-year-old woman lost her nineteen-year-old brother in a drowning accident. Slipping through the ice on Lake Superior, his body was not recovered until it washed up in a ravine on the banks of the lake. Living in another country at the time of his death, she was grieving, feeling lonely and disconnected. Anything but grateful. But then she discovered the following:

> One day on the way to work I noticed some people sitting under the shade of a big tree laughing and having a good time. Some did not have a leg, some no arms, some a patch on their eyes. Later, I learned these were people from a leper colony. I was struck that they were ostracized from their community, but they were enjoying life. At that moment, I started to become more grateful and humble. I was grateful for their gathering. I was thankful that I had two arms and two legs. I was starting to change. I started to be thankful for all that was and wasn't. I would make a conscious choice to change my line of thinking. My brother was not here anymore; I would no longer focus on the unfairness of his death. I was here. I had family. I had my life. My brother's death allowed me to see how precious life is.[15]

Remember, your goal is not to relive the experience but rather to get a new perspective on it. Simply rehearsing an upsetting event makes us feel worse about it. That is why catharsis has rarely been effective. Emotional venting without accompanying insight does not produce change. No amount of writing about the event will help unless you are able to take a fresh, redemptive perspective on it. This is an advantage that grateful people have, and it is a skill that can be learned no matter what your characteristic level of gratitude may be.

Why We Love Tear-Jerkers

A fascinating 2012 study conducted by researchers at the Ohio State University was designed to explain why we love tragic tales in books or movies. Why do we willingly subject ourselves, over and over, to movies such as *Ghost, Titanic, Anna Karenina*, and *Gone with the Wind*? Why is the tragedy genre so popular? Professor of communication Silvia Knobloch-Westerwick and her colleagues proposed the tragedy paradox: more sadness produces greater tragedy enjoyment. Participants watched an abridged version of the 2007 British film *Atonement,* starring Keira Knightley and James McAvoy. They noted that the film "depicts how a teenaged girl, Briony, accuses her sister's lover of a rape that he did not commit, which permanently changes the lives of all involved." Immediately before and after the showing, participants filled out detailed questionnaires measuring how they felt about their lives in general and how happy or sad they were feeling at the moment. The latter set of questions was also asked during three pauses embedded into the film. After the film they were asked to write about how the movie had led them to reflect on themselves, their goals, their relationships, and life in general. Even though the viewers found the film depressing, they were also more likely to endorse grateful appreciation as reflected in statements such as "the movie definitely made me appreciate what I have in life";

"it also makes me realize how blessed I am to have a life that is going great"; "the movie will make you appreciate what you have and how quickly it can be taken away"; "it makes me reflect on how to not take life for granted."[16] Vicarious exposure to tragedy can awaken dormant feelings of gratitude. Ironically, we may need to first get sad before we can get grateful. It's been said that for tragedy to be real, there must be something truly precious on the line. So gratitude is the flip side of tragedy, not despair or emptiness. These occur when there is no longer anything to live for or to die for.

Gratitude and Collective Trauma

Reframing shared trauma (for example, natural events such as hurricanes, earthquakes, and floods and human atrocities such as terrorist attacks and mass shootings) in order to unearth its redemptive qualities can be helpful for communities as well as for individuals. When parents who lived in south Florida at the time of Hurricane Andrew were interviewed, one of the key themes that emerged was an overwhelming sense of gratitude for what they had *not* lost during the hurricane. Although five of the families' homes had been so damaged that they had to relocate, none of them had lost a loved one. Because they were spared the loss of what was most important to them, they experienced profound gratitude in the midst of terrible disaster.

Another example of this kind of extraordinary emergence of gratitude in the midst of disaster occurred after the trio of disasters that struck Japan in March 2011. Miko Otomo was with her husband, three children, and her eighty-two-year-old father when the earthquake in Japan hit their home in Sendai. They managed to reach their car and sped to safety before the tsunami's black wall of water barreled through. "My older sister was in a bus when the wave came behind them. The bus driver told everybody to get out of the bus and run," said Ms. Otomo. "My sister was able to get away but some people just couldn't run fast enough.

"The tsunami wave was coming and I grabbed grandfather and our dog and drove. The wave was right behind me but I had to keep zigzagging around obstacles and the water to get to safety," Otomo told reporters. Ms. Otomo is grateful that her entire family was able to escape the wave.[17] One year after the tsunami and earthquake, singer-songwriter Tatsuya Ishi'i, a well-known performer in Japan, worked with children who had experienced the earthquake and tsunami. Mr. Ishi'i's project was to write a song compiled from the children's impressions or experiences during and after the disaster. After he set their contributions to music, he asked the class what they wanted to call the song. To his surprise, one student raised her hand and said, "*Sekai ni arigato*" ("Thank you for the world").[18]

Challenges don't always come in the form of unpleasant or unexpected events. In a study of new parents, researchers found that "reminding oneself of things for which to be grateful" was rated among the most helpful in coping with their newborns (after "doing things with the child," "being a parent to the baby," "and trusting in one's partner").[19]

Corroborating these findings, a recent study examining trauma history in college women revealed that gratitude (measured by a four-item posttrauma gratitude scale including *fortunate*, *grateful*, *appreciated life*, and *relieved*) was associated with emotional growth. For the worst event they had experienced, participants answered questions addressing whether the trauma involved threat of death, injury, or to physical integrity and whether they had felt extreme fear, helplessness, or horror. Women who retrospectively reported greater gratitude in response to trauma reported fewer and less-severe post-traumatic stress syndrome symptoms months and years after the event. The findings may suggest that gratitude is a protective factor for women. Perhaps the thinking associated with gratitude, such as a focus on benefits, are incompatible with those associated with psychopathology, such as self-blame. For example, movement from perception of victim to an agent was commonplace: "I am able to choose my own actions," "I focus my efforts on things that I can control."[20]

Some years ago I asked people with debilitating physical illnesses to compose a narrative concerning a time where they felt a deep sense of gratitude to someone or for something. I asked them to let themselves re-create that experience in their minds so that they could feel the emotions as if they had transported themselves back in time to the event itself. I also had them reflect on what they felt in that situation and how they expressed those feelings. In the face of progressive diseases, people often find life extremely challenging, painful, and frustrating. I wondered whether it would even be possible for them to find *anything* to be grateful about. For many of them, life revolved around visits to the pain clinic and pharmacy. I would not have at all been surprised if resentment overshadowed grate-fulness. As it turned out, most respondents had trouble settling on a specific instance—they simply had so much in their lives that they were grateful for. I was struck by the profound depth of feeling that they conveyed in their essays and by the apparent life-transforming power of gratitude in many of their lives. It was evident from reading these narrative accounts that (1) gratitude can be an overwhelmingly intense feeling, (2) gratitude for gifts that others easily overlook most can be the most powerful and frequent form of thankfulness, and (3) gratitude can be chosen in spite of one's situation or circumstances. I was also struck by the redemptive twist that occurred in nearly half of these narra-tives: out of something bad (suffering, adversity, affliction) came something good (new life or new opportunities) for which the person felt profoundly grateful.

A sixty-two-year-old woman with Charcot-Marie-Tooth disease (an inherited neuromuscular condition affecting the peripheral nerves) recounted horror story after horror story in our narratives-of-gratitude study. Fifteen years before, she fell backward and cracked her upper spine. She had emergency surgery and was told that the fall nearly severed her spinal cord and then spent twenty-nine days in the hospital. A short time after, her twenty-eight-year-old son was murdered. Two years later, her father died. She writes:

> My heart was so broken, I just couldn't understand
> why GOD would hurt me so when I was a good person
> and raised my children to be good people! I was hurting so

much I thought I would die. The next year, the same month and on my birthday, my daughter, who was born [on] Christmas, gave me a grand-daughter!!! My first grandchild . . . so after that I've never second guessed God ever! My younger son married in 1993 and didn't want a best man, because he said his best man was dead. Four years later he and his wife had twins, a boy and a girl. He named them Karlie Rae and Kyle William. The William was for his brother. I'm grateful and live each day with appreciation for life. I thank God each day, because without my family I would be so empty. Even though I'm not well and I hurt, I love life.[21]

Redemptive twists like these are stories of suffering and pain that turn into opportunities for celebration. The bad is redeemed into the good. The twist from the negative to the positive accounts for the power of the sequence—it is not just a happy ending. These are stories we love to hear about and love to tell about in our own lives. These are the stories that inspire and sustain. Who would fail to be inspired by a protagonist overcoming suffering and hardship? Psychologist Dan McAdams contends that the redemptive narrative is quintessentially American—from the lives of the Massachusetts Puritans and escaped African American slaves to the stories of release and recovery told in twelve-step programs, from the pulpit, and in Hollywood.[22] The possibility exists that each of us can find redemption. Surveying US novels and short stories from recent years, the *New York Times* book reviewer Michiko Kakutani wrote, "There is no public narrative more potent today—or throughout American history—than the one about redemption."[23]

Gratitude in the Midst of Grief

Chaplain Timothy VanDuivendyck is the vice president of spiritual care at the massive Memorial Hermann Healthcare System in Houston. I met Tim a few years ago when he invited me to be the keynote speaker at their annual conference on pastoral care. His book, *The Unwanted Gift of Grief*, is a compassionate resource for people who have suffered loss to help guide them through the grieving process. His central thesis is that when we express grief for our loved one, we are expressing gratitude for him or her. The pain of loss—the sadness, depression, the emptiness, the longing that we feel are really expressions of gratitude. It's an amazing perspective that can really help us process the mixture of feelings in the aftermath of a loss.[24]

One of my favorite movies of all time is *Shadowlands*, in which Oxford professor C. S. Lewis (played by Anthony Hopkins) meets and marries Joy Gresham (Debra Winger), only to lose her to cancer. At one point, Joy wants to speak to him about her illness and imminent death, and Lewis, of course, objects. But, she tells him that pain and happiness are tied together, that the pain of the present moment is made possible only by past happiness. After losing Joy, he comes to this realization himself as he remembers that the pain now is part of the happiness then. We might add that the grief now is part of the gratitude now. That's the deal.

Here are some ways in which you might experience gratitude in the midst of grief. Think about what you have learned from the person who died. What life lessons were passed on? How many smiles did that person give you? How many times did he or she cause you to laugh? Or how many meals and good times did you have together? Who taught you how to be a parent, son or daughter, or how to talk to strangers? Who comforted you when you were sick? Who did you take long walks with? Who taught you how to throw a baseball or ride a bike? Who gave you joy? You can be grateful for all these gifts even as you mourn the loss of the person who gave them to you. You may even want to write a thank-you letter. Remembering is a way to honor your loved one and keep him or her in your life.

This morning I learned of the loss of a friend and colleague, Chris Peterson of the University of Michigan. Chris was a giant in the field of positive psychology who died unexpectedly and much too young. Stunning as the news was, I asked myself, what better time to practice what I preach? I thought about what I had learned from Chris. I first met him when I interviewed for a job at the University of Michigan in the late 1980s. For a young assistant professor, an interview in a top department at a prestigious university is a nerve-wracking experience. Chris was on the search committee, and I'll never forget how comfortable he made me feel at the dinner the night before my job talk. In the two-plus decades after this experience, we traveled in many of the same professional circles. He was always gracious, kind, warm, and generous with his time, qualities that can be in short supply in the competitive world of academia. He was the editor of my groundbreaking study on the benefits of gratitude journaling, taking over from the original editor who let my paper languish on his desk for nearly two years. Chris accepted the paper immediately. He brought me into the inner circle of positive psychology heavyweights and helped me gain an editorship of the first journal of positive psychology to which he made major contributions. I could go on and on. I understand what it means to say there is gratitude in grief. In our grief for our lost loved one, we are expressing our gratitude for him or her.

* GRATEFUL FOR EVERYTHING *

Life inevitably offers a mixture of good and bad times, victories and defeats, agonies and ecstasies, joys and sorrows. Haven't we all seen people whose lives reflect resilience and hope in the face of histories of formidable losses and adversity, and others who manifest chronic sadness and regret even though they've benefitted from good fortune and privilege? Surely there are prevailing differences in temperament that account for some of the differences we see between people in their levels of gratitude. But our current emotional state greatly hinges on what we are using as our frame of reference.

An outstanding example of the use of gratitude as a frame of reference can be seen in the life of Alice Herz-Sommer, the oldest survivor of the Holocaust and the second-oldest person living in London, England. At the time I write this she is 108. Alice was a renowned concert pianist and a close friend of

Franz Kafka. She has seen and lived through more than any of us can imagine. And despite of all she's experienced, her extraordinary optimism and attitude are what stand out the most. In 1942, Alice was a well-known concert pianist living in Prague. At age thirty-nine, she was deported to Theresienstadt, a Nazi concentration camp. For propaganda purposes, Theresienstadt was the only camp in which children were not taken from their parents. Alice had been deported with her little boy, Raffi. Designed by the Nazis to deceive the international community, its purpose was to show the world how well the Jews of Europe were being treated by their Nazi captors. Under constant threat of extermination, starving prisoners were permitted to paint, perform, and make music. In Theresienstadt, Alice gave more than one hundred concerts, performing all of Chopin's etudes from memory, which is the reason she was permitted to survive. Alice's faith and inspiration were passed on to her son, Raffi, who sang in the Theresienstadt's children's opera, Brundibar. Alice's undiminished optimism gave him strength, and he too survived.

Remarkably, she still lives in the same apartment she has lived in for many years and still plays the piano. To the residents of this small apartment building in north London, Alice Herz-Sommer is simply the woman in number six. One resident said, "One of the benefits of living in this block is having classical music beautifully played morning and afternoon. In fact, I know people who just stand outside the building in the street listening to her and just admiring her playing. And she still plays every day."

Alice receives visitors every afternoon, people who come to hear her stories and learn from her experience. At age 104 she even wrote a book titled *A Garden of Eden in Hell.*

Here are some quotes from interviews available on YouTube:

- "I am Jewish but Beethoven is my religion. Music saved my life and music saves me still. My world is music."
- "I have had such a beautiful life. And life is beautiful, love is beautiful, nature and music are beautiful. Everything we experience is a gift, a present we should cherish and pass on to those we love."
- "I love people. I love everyone. I love to speak with them. I'm interested in the lives of other people."
- "I was born optimistic. And this helps you. When you are optimistic, when you are not complaining, when you look at the good side of your life, everybody loves you."

When one interviewer asked her if she ever felt pain when she was in the Nazi camp, she simply replied, "No pain. I was always laughing." An interviewer commented, "You focused on the good. This is how you made your life work." She replied, "My mother taught me to learn, learn, learn—know, know, know—think, think, think. I learned to be grateful for everything. I am thankful and happy every day." Alice Hertz-Sommer has lived a life that was enhanced by the unquench-able power of music as well as her everyday feelings of being happy and grateful for everything. She remains a beacon of hope and inspiration to everyone who knows her. She has her health, her friends, and her music. At 108, she feels she's one of the luckiest people alive.

"In any case, life is beautiful, extremely beautiful. And when you are old you appreciate it more. When you are older you think, you remember, you care, and you appreciate. You are thankful for everything. For everything."[25]

7

The
Twenty-One-Day
Gratitude Challenge

The previous chapters lead us to the final stage in our journey: the twenty-one-day gratitude challenge. Unless we are able to make the practices that I have presented work for us, the discussion remains purely theoretical, having no noticeable impact on our lives. If you have read this far, then you are interested in becoming a more grateful person. This final chapter is designed with you in mind.

The first step in the gratitude challenge is to assess, in a general way, how grateful you are now. There is no judgment implied in this assessment; it's simply meant to give you a benchmark so that you can see how the journaling exercises and other tools I have given you in the previous chapters can change your attitudes and feelings over the next twenty-one days.

HOW GRATEFUL ARE YOU? TEST YOUR GRATITUDE QUOTIENT

1 = strongly disagree

2 = disagree

3 = slightly disagree

4 = neutral

5 = slightly agree

6 = agree

7 = strongly agree

____ 1. I have so much in life to be thankful for.

____ 2. If I had to list everything that I felt grateful for, it would be a very long list.

____ 3. When I look at the world, I don't see much to be grateful for.

____ 4. I am grateful to a wide variety of people.

____ 5. As I get older I find myself more able to appreciate the people, events, and situations that have been part of my life history.

____ 6. Long amounts of time can go by before I feel grateful to something or someone.

____ 7. I have been richly blessed in my life.

____ 8. To be honest, it takes an awful lot to make a person like me feel appreciative.

____ 9. I have a wonderful sense of thanksgiving for life itself.

____10. I often reflect on how much easier my life is because of the efforts of others.[1]

How to Calculate Your Score

1. Add up your scores for items 1, 2, 4, 5, 7, 9, and 10.
2. Reverse your scores for items 3, 6, and 8. That is, if you scored a 7, give yourself a 1, if you scored a 6, give yourself a 2, and so on.
3. Add the reversed scores for items 3, 6, and 8 to the total from step 1. This is your total gratitude quotient score. This number should be between 10 and 70.

How to Interpret Your Score

65-70: Extremely high gratitude. People who score in this range have the ability to see life as a gift. For you, gratitude is a way of life.

59-64: Very high gratitude. Your life contains frequent expressions of gratitude and you are able to readily acknowledge how others have helped you. The next twenty-one days will nevertheless help you recognize and enhance your gratefulness in every area of your life.

53-58: High gratitude. You are above average in gratitude and find it relatively easy to spend time reflecting on your blessings. You will probably find much to enjoy in the next twenty-one days.

46-52: Average gratitude. You may find it easy being grateful when things are going well in your life but may have difficulties maintaining a grateful outlook in tough times. You may find good value in gratitude journaling and the other practices over the next twenty-one days.

40–45: Below average gratitude. You find it challenging to find reasons for gratitude in your life. Life is more of a burden than a gift. Perhaps you are just going through a downturn. But if that's not the case, going through the journaling exercises over the next twenty-one days may make a difference in the way you see the world and live your life.

* OVERVIEW OF THE TWENTY-ONE-DAY CHALLENGE *

At the heart of the twenty-one-day gratitude challenge is the practice of keeping a gratitude journal. Your journal will become a permanent record that is a gift to yourself and can inspire you to a deeper realization that life is a continual invitation to gratitude. In the pages that follow you will find seven separate sets of exercises, one for each day of the week for the next three weeks. Over the next twenty-one days, the challenge is that you complete each gratitude exercise three different times in your journal. Please try them all, even if you discover that some practices personally work better for you. You'll want to buy a notebook or journal—it doesn't have to be fancy—in which to record your entries. Be sure to date and label each entry so that its title matches the one in the exercise; that way you can keep track of your growth and change over time.

On the first day, you will follow the instructions for "the three blessings" exercise. You will repeat this exercise on days eight and fifteen. On days two, nine, and sixteen, turn your attention to "to whom for what." The exercise for days three, ten, and seventeen asks that you focus on the gifts that you have received this day. On days four, eleven, and eighteen, you will select something positive from your life that will be ending in the relatively near future. The fifth exercise (days five, twelve, and nineteen) asks you to think about a positive event or experience and how it might not have occurred in your life. Days six, thirteen, and twenty ask that you compose and deliver a brief gratitude letter to someone in your life. The final exercise (days seven, fourteen, and twenty-one) asks you to "remember the bad." See figure 7.1.

Day One: The Three Blessings

Day Two: To Whom for What

Day Three: The Gifted Self

Day Four: Scarcity

Day Five: Absence of Blessing

Day Six: The Gratitude Letter

Day Seven: Remember the Bad

Figure 7.1   Seven Gratitude Practices

As you cycle through the exercises each week, you should make sure each time through that you vary what you write about. For example, in the gratitude letter, choose three different people on those three days.

Each day, set aside a period of about ten minutes to write your journal entry that matches the category for that day. Don't be too rigid. Take as much time as you need. Even when you don't think you have anything interesting to say, honor that commitment and write something. Becoming more grateful is an exercise in training one's mind and training requires

	Week 1 Day 1 Sunday	Week 1 Day 2 Monday	Week 1 Day 3 Tuesday	Week 1 Day 4 Wednesday	Week 1 Day 5 Thursday	Week 1 Day 6 Friday	Week 1 Day 7 Saturday
The Three Blessings	X						
To Whom for What		X					
The Gifted Self			X				
Scarcity				X			
Absence of Blessing					X		
The Gratitude Letter						X	
Remember the Bad							X

Figure 7.2   Weekly Gratitude Journaling

practice. You are likely to find that the exercises become easier as you practice them more intentionally and deliberately over the next twenty-one days. You will get better at it! If you need, go back and read the sections of chapters 2 and 3 that are relevant to the assigned exercise for the day. The suggestions that I have given in these chapters and elsewhere should help you.

Figure 7.2 graphically shows the pattern to follow in your twenty-one-day journey. Your task is to distribute the entries across the categories so that by the end of the week, you will have explored all the different prompts to enhance gratitude in your life. This particular chart begins the week on a Sunday and ends on a Saturday; you can choose your own beginning and ending days.

* THREE BLESSINGS: DAYS ONE, EIGHT, AND FIFTEEN *

Spend a few minutes recalling and writing down three good things that happened today for which you could give other people some credit. Someone complimented you on your appearance, a colleague helped you make significant progress on a project that had become bogged down, an old friend whom you had not heard from in years contacted you. These things can be anything that went well, both the big and the small in your life. They do not have to be spectacular or dramatic. It is important to write down why that good thing happened. What enabled the positive event? Why do you think it happened? What does it mean to you? What can you do to make it happen again? Did you tell anyone about the good thing?

Write some words down that describe or remind you of the positive experience, then follow up with some reflection on why that particular experience went well. Think of as many reasons as you can. Then think about a second thing that happened today that went well, write it down, and reflect why. Then think about a third good thing, write it down, and reflect why. It is very important for you to write down at least a couple of words on why things went well because it helps you to again experience the good things that happened during your day. Even if these things are small and trivial, such as a smile or enjoying a moment of relaxation, they are good things and that is what is important to focus on. Spend about ten minutes on this exercise.

* TO WHOM FOR WHAT? DAYS TWO, NINE, AND SIXTEEN *

There is a difference between feeling grateful *about something* and feeling grateful *to someone*. Brother David Steindl-Rast distinguishes between thankfulness and gratefulness. Thankfulness, for Brother David, is a much more personal experience that occurs when we have benefitted from a specific kindness from another person.[2] To say that one is thankful to someone and grateful for something seems to be the more commonly preferred usage. More significant is the fact that thanking and thinking are cognates. To thank originally meant to think of a gift and has come to mean the feeling aroused by these thoughts and their expression in a thankful attitude.

When we thank, we think—namely in terms of giver, gift, and receiver. This exercise is designed to stimulate a sense of thankfulness.

Many circumstances or events can elicit thankfulness but it is most often a response to a benefit received from another person or God. In this activity you will focus on those things in your life that you might be grateful or thankful for and the source or provider of these good things. Who has provided you with a benefit? Your spouse? A neighbor? Coworker? One of your students? Your favorite sports team? Think back over the day and write down up to five things for which you are thankful and who provided this gift or benefit to you. You can use this format:

* * *

I am grateful to _____ for
_____.

* THE GIFTED SELF: DAYS THREE, TEN, AND SEVENTEEN *

In this activity you will focus for a moment on benefits or "gifts" that you have received in your life. These gifts could be simple everyday pleasures, people in your life, personal strengths or talents, moments of natural beauty, or gestures of kindness from others. We might not usually think about these things as gifts, but that is how I want you to think about them. Slowly repeat the word *gift* or a phrase such as *I am gifted* or *I have been gifted* several times. Be aware of your feelings and how you relish and savor this gift in your imagination. Take the time to be aware especially of the depth of your gratitude. Contemplate the value of these gifts and then write them down in your journal.

There is a second part to this exercise. Receiving a gift often ignites a desire to reciprocate. Ask yourself the question, "In what ways might I give back to others as an appropriate response for the gratitude I feel?" Be creative. Is there a way that you can pass along the gift to others? Can you "pay it forward"? Who can you tell about this gift you received? Can you perform a nonrandom act of kindness? Offer to pay for the person's coffee behind you in line, toll for the automobile behind you at the toll plaza, or car behind you in the fast-food drive-thru? Maybe there is an elderly person in your neighborhood who might need assistance with grocery shopping, errands, or other household chores. Put some coins in a meter that is about to expire. Help someone who appears to be lost. Teach a skill to a child. The list is endless. Passing on the gift is the best way to demonstrate gratitude for it.

* LOOKING TO THE FUTURE: DAYS FOUR, ELEVEN, AND EIGHTEEN *

As I have discussed, when people believe that a positive life event is about to end, they are more likely to appreciate it more and make more of an effort to capitalize on the remaining time. A sense of "now or never" can impel us to make the most of every day.

In this exercise, choose an activity, event, experience, or relationship (let's call it x) that may be ending soon. Keep in mind that you only have a short amount of time left to spend doing x or being with x. Maybe it's a job that you have, a class that you are taking, a team that you are on, or a place where you are living. This chapter of your life will end soon. Try to select an experience in which you have between one and three months remaining. Given how little time you have left with x, write about why you are grateful for x.

* THE ABSENCE OF BLESSING: DAYS FIVE, TWELVE, AND NINETEEN *

In gratitude, we think about and affirm the good. But there are many ways to think about the good things in our lives and each may not have the same power to kindle grateful feelings. For this exercise, think about how a positive event or experience in your life might never have happened or might never have been part of your life. You can think of this as the "more by less" phenomenon. By taking something away in our minds, we become more aware of benefits that we still have but previously took for granted. Mentally subtracting something good from your life can make you more grateful for it.

Think of an aspect of your life for which you feel grateful and then write about the ways in which this might never have happened (e.g., "what would have happened if I had never met my wife?" as opposed to "I am so grateful to have met my wife").

* THE GRATITUDE LETTER: DAYS SIX, THIRTEEN, AND TWENTY *

It is said that feeling gratitude but not expressing it is like wrapping a present and not giving it. For various reasons, we often don't express gratitude to those who deserve our thanks. We assume they know how much we appreciate them. We felt that they were only doing their job, not realizing that this does not alleviate us of the need to let them know. We planned to but somehow never got around to it. Too much time has passed and we feel embarrassed by our forgetfulness.

In this activity, remember a time in your life when you were grateful for something that another person did for you and then write a letter to that person. Was it a teacher, mentor, coach, close personal friend? It is up to you whether you send the letter or not. In the letter, describe specifically why you are grateful to this person, how he or she affected your life, and how often you reflect on his or her efforts. What did he or she do and how does that still affect your life? This should be someone whom you have never properly taken the time to thank and could be a parent, teacher, friend, relative, coach, or someone else. You can compose it using whatever medium (stationary, e-mail, video) that you feel comfortable with. Spend at least ten to fifteen minutes on this letter. Your letter should be around 250 words. Whether or not you actually send it, imagine how reading the letter will make the recipient feel.

* BAD TO GOOD: DAYS SEVEN, FOURTEEN, AND TWENTY-ONE *

One strategy for cultivating gratitude is to "remember the bad." Think of your worst moments, your sorrows, your losses, and your sadness and then remember. Focus on how you got through the worst day of your life, the trauma, the trial; you endured the temptation; you survived the bad relationship; you're making your way out of the dark. Remember the bad things and then look to see where you are now.

The seventh daily exercise involves a variation on this strategy. Sometimes even when bad things happen they can ultimately have positive consequences, things we can now be grateful for. Choose an experience from your life that was initially unpleasant and unwanted. Try now to focus on the positive aspects or consequences of this difficult experience. As the result of this event, what kinds of things do you now feel thankful or grateful for? Has this event benefited you as a person? How have you grown? Were there personal strengths that grew out of your experience? How has the event made you better able to meet the challenges of the future? How has the event put your life into perspective? How has the event helped you appreciate the truly important people and things in your life? In sum, how can you be thankful for the beneficial consequences that have resulted from this event? Try to write about three different unpleasant events on days seven, fourteen, and twenty-one.

* REFLECTIONS *

Now that you have completed the twenty-one-day challenge, please spend some time reflecting on the following questions. Write about them in the journal if you wish. Your reactions are a valuable aspect of this entire experience.

- What have you learned about yourself?
- Which exercise most resonated with you?
- Which exercises were most difficult?
- As you took the challenge, what did you find surprising?
- What obstacles and roadblocks did you encounter over the twenty-one days?
- How did you overcome these obstacles?
- Do you plan to continue journaling? Why or why not?
- Have you found other journaling practices that have sparked gratitude in you?
- Have you shared these practices with anyone?
- Do you believe that you have become a more grateful person?

I would love to receive your feedback on what you found effective and what you did not. More generally, I would love to hear about what gratitude means to you. Please feel free to contact me at raemmons@ucdavis.edu or write to me at the Department of Psychology, University of California, One Shields Avenue, Davis, CA 95616. Make gratitude work for you!

Notes

Preface
1. Howard Becker, *Man in Reciprocity* (Westport, CT: Greenwood Press, 1973), 226.
2. Edward J. Harpham, "Gratitude in the History of Ideas," in *The Psychology of Gratitude*, ed. Robert A. Emmons and Michael E. McCullough (New York: Oxford University Press), 19.
3. Ibid., 20.

Chapter One: The Challenge of Gratitude
1. Personal communication (January 2011).
2. Alex M. Wood, Jeffrey J. Froh, and Adam W. A. Geraghty, "Gratitude and Well-Being: A Review and Theoretical Integration," *Clinical Psychology Review* (2010): 890–905.
3. Rick Hanson, *Buddha's Brain: The Practical Neuroscience of Happiness, Love, and Wisdom* (Berkeley, CA: New Harbinger Publications, 2009).
4. Rollin McCraty and Doc Childre, "The Grateful Heart: The Psychophysiology of Appreciation," in *The Psychology of*

Gratitude, ed. R. A. Emmons and M. E. McCullough (New York: Oxford University Press, 2004), 230–255.

5. Stephen G. Post, *Why Good Things Happen to Good People* (New York: Broadway, 2007), 32.

6. Robert A. Emmons, *Thanks! How the New Science of Gratitude Can Make You Happier* (Boston: Houghton-Mifflin, 2007).

7. Personal communication (December 2011).

8. Emmons (2007).

9. Robert A. Emmons and Anjali Mishra, "Gratitude," in *Religion, Spirituality, and Positive Psychology: Understanding the Psychological Fruits of Faith*, ed. Thomas G. Plante (Santa Barbara, CA: Praeger), 9–30.

10. Michael F. Steger, Brian M. Hicks, Todd B. Kashdan, Robert F. Krueger, and Thomas J. Bouchard Jr., "Genetic and Environmental Influences on the Positive Traits of the Values in Action Classification, and Biometric Covariance with Normal Personality," *Journal of Research in Personality*, 41 (2007): 524–539.

Chapter Two: Journaling for Gratitude

1. Personal communication (November 2010).

2. Jack Kornfield, *The Wise Heart: A Guide to the Universal Teachings of Buddhist Psychology* (New York: Bantam, 2009), 400.

3. Robert A. Emmons and Michael E. McCullough, "Counting Blessings Versus Burdens: An Experimental Investigation of Gratitude and Subjective Well-Being in Daily Life," *Journal of Personality and Social Psychology*, 84 (2003): 377–389.

4. Ibid.

5. Shelley E. Taylor, "Adjustment to Threatening Events: A Theory of Cognitive Adaptation," *American Psychologist*, 38 (1983): 1161–1173.

6. David Steindl-Rast, "A Good Day," www.gratefulness.org /brotherdavid/a-good-day.htm.

7. Angeles Arrien, *Living in Gratitude: A Journey That Will Change Your Life* (Boulder, CO: Sounds True, 2011).

8. La Rochefoucauld, *Moral Reflections, Part I*, www.bartleby .com/350/4.html.

9. Gregg Krech, *Naikan: Gratitude, Grace, and the Japanese Art of Self-Reflection* (Berkeley, CA: Stone Bridge Press, 2002).

10. Ravi Iyer and Carlyn Carter, *Exploring the Optimal Gratitude Practice: Depth, Quantity, and Personalization*, unpublished manuscript, University of Southern California, Los Angeles (2009).

11. Andrew Ortony, Gerald L. Clore, and Allan Collins, *The Cognitive Structure of the Emotions* (New York: Cambridge University Press, 1988).

12. Gilbert K. Chesterton, *St. Francis of Assisi* (Mineola, NY: Dover Publications, 2008), 71.

13. Minkyung Koo, Sara B. Algoe, Timothy D. Wilson, and Daniel T. Gilbert, "It's a Wonderful Life: Subtracting Positive Events Improves People's Affective States, Contrary to Their Affective Forecasts," *Journal of Personality and Social Psychology, 95* (2008): 1217–1224.

14. Nico H. Frijda, "The Laws of Emotion," *American Psychologist, 43* (1988): 349–358. Quote from p. 350.

15. Koo, Algoe, Wilson, and Gilbert (2008).

16. *The Works of Samuel Johnson*, vol. 6 (London: W. Bynes and Son, 1818/2010), 271.

17. Jaime L. Kurtz, "Looking to the Future to Appreciate the Present: The Benefits of Perceived Temporal Scarcity," *Psychological Science, 19* (2008): 1238–1241.

18. Winifred Gallagher, *New: Understanding Our Need for Novelty and Change* (New York: The Penguin Press, 2012).

19. C. Robert Cloninger, *Feeling Good: The Science of Well-Being* (New York: Oxford University Press, 2004).

20. Sonja Lyubomirsky, Kennon Sheldon, and David Schkade, "Pursuing Happiness: The Architecture of Sustainable Change," *Review of General Psychology*, 9 (2005): 111–131.

21. Michael J. Fox, *Always Looking Up: The Adventures of an Incurable Optimist* (New York: Hyperion, 2009), 201.

22. Patrick McNamara, *Where God and Science Meet: The Neurology of Religious Experience* (Westport, CT: Praeger, 2006).

23. F. Gregory Ashby, Alice M. Isen, and U. Turken, "A Neuropsychological Theory of Positive Affect and Its Influence on Cognition," *Psychological Review*, 106 (1999): 529–550.

Chapter Three: Beyond the Journal

1. Gertrude Stein, www.quotationspage.com/quote/32983.html

2. Walter Green, *This Is the Moment: How One Man's Year-Long Journey Captured the Power of Extraordinary Gratitude* (Carlsbad, CA: Hay House, 2010).

3. Edward Hoffman, ed., *Future Visions: The Unpublished Papers of Abraham Maslow* (Thousand Oaks, CA: Sage, 1996), 78.

4. Martin E. P. Seligman, *Authentic Happiness: Using the New Positive Psychology to Realize Your Potential for Lasting Fulfillment* (New York: The Free Press, 2002), 74.

5. Martin E. P. Seligman, Tracy A. Steen, Nansook Park, and Christopher Peterson, "Positive Psychology Progress: Empirical Validation of Interventions," *American Psychologist*, 60 (2005): 410–421.

6. Philip C. Watkins, Kathrane Woodward, Tamara Stone, and Russell L. Koltz, "Gratitude and Happiness: Development of a Measure of Gratitude and Relationships with Subjective Well-Being," *Social Behavior and Personality*, 31 (2003): 431–452.

7. Steven M. Toepfer and Kathleen Walker, "Letters of Gratitude: Improving Well-Being Through Expressive Writing," *Journal of Writing Research*, 1 (2009): 181–198.

8. Steven M. Toepfer, Kelly Clehy, and Patti Peters, "Letters of Gratitude: Further Evidence for Author Benefits," *Journal of Happiness Studies*, 1 (2012): 187–201.

9. Matthew T. Lieberman, Naomi I. Eisenberger, Molly J. Crockett, Sabrina M. Tom, Jennifer H. Pfiefer, and Baldwin M. Way, "Putting Feelings into Words: Affect Labeling Disrupts Amygdala Activity in Response to Affective Stimuli," *Psychological Science*, 18 (2007): 421–428.

10. Dorothy C. Bass, *Practicing Our Faith: A Way of Life for a Searching People* (New York: Wiley, 2010), 92.

11. David Hochman, "How to Be Thankful and Improve Your Life," *Readers Digest* (2009): 163–166. Quote from p. 166.

12. John Mackey, "Bentley College Commencement Speech," www.wholefoodsmarket.com/blog/john-mackeys-blog/bentley-college-commencement%C2%A0speech.

13. Moira Clark, "Bosses Are Worse at Saying Thank You to Staff Than 10 Years Ago," *CallcentreHelper.com*, www.callcentrehelper.com/bosses-are-worse-at-saying-thank-you-to-staff-than-10-years-ago-2226.htm.

14. Ibid.

15. Howard Jacobson, *Gratitude as a Business Strategy* (November 23, 2011), www.fastcompany.com/1796660/gratitude-business-strategy.

16. Bruce Rind and Prashant Bordia, "Effect of Server's 'Thank You' and Personalization on Restaurant Tipping," *Journal of Applied Social Psychology*, 25 (1995): 745–751.

17. J. Ronald Carey, Stephen H. Clicque, Barbara A. Leighton, and Frank Milton, "A Test of Positive Reinforcement of Customers," *Journal of Marketing*, 40 (1976): 98–100.

18. Natalia Kolyesnikova and Tim H. Dodd, "Effects of Winery Visitor Group Size on Gratitude and Obligation," *Journal of Travel Research*, 47 (2008): 104–112.

19. Randle Raggio and Judith A. Garretson, "Expressions of Gratitude in Disaster Management: An Economic, Social Marketing, and Public Policy Perspective on Post-Katrina Campaigns," *Journal of Public Policy and Marketing*, 30 (2011): 168–174.

20. Margaret Visser, *The Gift of Thanks: The Roots, Persistence, and Paradoxical Meanings of a Social Ritual* (Toronto: HarperCollins, 2008), 10.

21. Jeffrey J. Froh, Giacomo Bono, Robert A. Emmons, and Kathleen Henderson, "Nice Thinking! An Educational Intervention That Teaches Children How to Think Gratefully," *School Psychology Review* (in press).

22. Ibid.

23. Ibid.

24. Jeffrey J. Froh, Todd Kashdan, Kathleen M. Ozimkowski, and Norman Miller, "Who Benefits the Most from a Gratitude Intervention in Children and Adolescents? Examining Positive Affect as a Moderator," *Journal of Positive Psychology*, 4 (2009): 408–422.

25. Ibid.

26. C. Everett Koop, *Koop: The Memoirs of America's Family Doctor* (New York: Random House, 1991), 109.

27. Elizabeth Bibesco, www.quoteworld.org/quotes/1344.

Chapter Four: Growing Gratitude Through Spiritual Disciplines
1. Dallas Willard, *The Spirit of the Disciplines: Understanding How God Changes Lives* (San Francisco: HarperOne, 1990).
2. Dallas Willard, "Spiritual Disciplines, Spiritual Formation, and the Restoration of the Soul," *Journal of Psychology and Theology*, 26 (1998): 102.
3. Willard, *The Spirit of the Disciplines*, 179.
4. David Steindl-Rast, *Gratitude as Thankfulness and as Gratefulness*, in Emmons and McCullough (2004), 283.
5. Robin McKie, "Fasting Can Help Protect Against Brain Diseases, Scientists Say," *The Observer* (February 18, 2012), www.guardian.co.uk/society/2012/feb/18/fasting-protect-brain-diseases-scientists.
6. Lauren Winner, *Mudhouse Sabbath: An Invitation to a Life of Spiritual Discipline* (Brewster, MA: Paraclete, 2008), 83.
7. Michael Zigarelli, "Gratitude: Pathway to Permanent Change," *Christianity 9 to 5*, www.epiphanyresources.com/9to5/articles/gratitude.htm.
8. Henri Nouwen, *Making All Things New: An Invitation to the Spiritual Life* (San Francisco: HarperOne, 1981), 69.
9. Richard J. Foster, *Celebration of Discipline: The Path to Spiritual Growth* (San Francisco: HarperOne, 1978).
10. John A. Simpson and Edmund S. Weiner, eds., *The Compact Oxford English Dictionary* (New York: Oxford University Press, 1991), 977.
11. Christopher R. Long and James R. Averill, "Solitude: An Exploration of Benefits of Being Alone," *Journal for the Theory of Social Behavior*, 33 (2003): 21–44.

12. Ibid., 23.

13. Ibid., 27.

14. Ibid., 33.

15. Jonathan Edwards, *A Treatise Concerning Religious Affections* (New York: American Tract Society, 1850), 245.

16. Timothy Kasser, *The High Price of Materialism* (Cambridge, MA: MIT Press, 2003).

17. Robert Emmons, unpublished study.

18. Ian J. Norris and Jeff T. Larsen, "Wanting More Than You Have and Its Consequences for Well-Being," *Journal of Happiness Studies*, 12 (2011): 887–885.

19. Michael Sacasas, "Gratitude as a Measure of Technology," *The Frailest Thing* (November 24, 2011), http://thefrailestthing.com/2011/11/24/gratitude-as-a-measure-of-technology.

20. St. Augustine, *Confessions*, trans. Henry Chadwick (New York: Oxford University Press, 2009), 186.

21. Seneca, "We Should Every Night . . . ," http://havingcourage tochange.blogspot.com/2012_09_01_archive.html.

22. In Gregg Krech, *Naikan: Gratitude, Grace, and the Japanese Art of Self-Reflection* (Berkeley, CA: Stone Bridge Press, 2002), 92.

23. Ibid, 31.

24. Paul Tillich, *The Shaking of the Foundations* (New York: Charles Scribner's Sons, 1948), 162.

Chapter Five: The Biggest Obstacle to Gratitude—and Its Remedy

1. Keith J. Campbell, "Psychological Entitlement: Interpersonal Consequences and Validation of a Self-Report Measure," *Journal of Personality Assessment*, 83 (2004): 29–45.

2. Mark E. Jonas, "Gratitude, *Ressentiment*, and Citizenship Education," *Studies in Philosophy and Education*, 31 (2012): 29–46.

3. Roger Scruton, "Gratitude and Grace," *American Spectator* (April 2010), spectator.org/archives/2010/04/02/gratitude-and-grace.

4. Stephen Schwarz, *Values and Human Experience: Essays in Honor of the Memory of Balduin Schwarz* (New York: P. Lang, 1999), 184.

5. Jean Twenge and Keith J. Campbell, *The Narcissism Epidemic: Living in the Age of Entitlement* (New York: Free Press, 2010).

6. Ellen Greenberger, J. Lessard, C. Chen, and S. P. Farruggia, "Self-Entitled College Students: Contributions of Personality, Parenting, and Motivational Factors," *Journal of Youth and Adolescence*, 37 (2008): 1193–1204.

7. Arlie Hochschild, *The Second Shift: Working Families and the Revolution at Home* (New York: Viking, 1989).

8. Dacher Keltner, Jeremy Smith, and Jason Marsh, *The Compassionate Instinct: The Science of Human Goodness* (New York: W. W. Norton, 2010), 113.

9. Stephanie Coontz, *Marriage, a History: How Love Conquered Marriage* (New York: Penguin, 2006), 261.

10. Julie J. Exline, "Modesty and Humility," in *Character Strengths and Virtues*, ed. Christopher Peterson and Martin E. P. Seligman (Washington, DC: American Psychological Association, 2002), 461–476.

11. Alan Morinis, *Everyday Holiness: The Jewish Spiritual Path of Mussar* (Boston: Shambhala, 2007), 48.

12. Julie J. Exline and Peter C. Hill, "Humility: A Consistent and Robust Predictor of Generosity," *Journal of Positive Psychology*, 7 (2012): 208–218.

13. Mark T. Mitchell, "Why I Am a Conservative," *First Principles* (September 29, 2008), www.firstprinciplesjournal.com/articles.aspx?articlev183&themevhome&locvb.

14. Alasdair MacIntyre, *Dependent Rational Animals: Why Human Beings Need the Virtues* (Chicago: Open Court, 2001).

15. Ursula Goodenough, *The Sacred Depths of Nature* (New York: Oxford University Press, 1998), 86.

16. Steve Cady, "A Brash Captain Keeps the Cup," *New York Times* (September 18, 1977), www.nytimes.com/packages/html/sports /year_in_sports/09.18.html.

17. Paul Wong, "I'm Glad That I'm a Nobody: A Positive Psychology of Humility" (November 2003), www.meaning.ca/archives /presidents_columns/pres_col_nov_2003.htm.

18. American Chesterton Society. *What's Wrong with the World*, www.chesterton.org/discover-chesterton/frequently-asked-ques tions/wrong-with-world.

19. McCraty and Childre (2004), 231.

20. Shimon Levy, *Theatre and the Holy Script* (Eastbourne, UK: Sussex Academic Press, 1999), 228–229.

Chapter Six: Gratitude, Suffering, and Redemption

1. M. Scott Peck, *The Road Less Traveled: A New Psychology of Love, Traditional Values and Spiritual Growth* (New York: Simon & Schuster, 1978).

2. Deborah C. Stevens, ed., *The Maslow Business Reader* (New York: John Wiley & Sons, 2010), 298.

3. Personal communication (March 2008).

4. Mary Chapin Carpenter, "The Learning Curve of Gratitude," in Jay Allison and Dan Gediman, eds., *This I Believe: The Personal Philosophies of Remarkable Men and Women* (New York: Holt, 2007), 44–46.

5. Peter J. Gomes, *The Good Life: Truths That Last in Times of Need* (San Francisco: HarperOne, 2003), 151.

6. Nico H. Frijda, "The Laws of Emotion," *American Psychologist*, 43 (1988): 349–358.

7. Araceli Frias, Philip C. Watkins, Amy C. Webber, and Jeffrey J. Froh, "Death and Gratitude: Death Reflection Enhances Gratitude," *Journal of Positive Psychology*, 6 (2011): 154–162.

8. Ibid, 161.

9. Dietrich Bonhoeffer, *Letters and Papers from Prison* (New York: Touchstone, 1997), 176.

10. Barbara Held, "The Negative Side of Positive Psychology," *Journal of Humanistic Psychology*, 44 (2004): 9–46.

11. Miriam Greenspan, *Healing Through the Dark Emotions: The Wisdom of Grief, Fear, and Despair* (Boston: Shambhala Publications, 2004), 1.

12. Philip C. Watkins, "Taking Care of Business? Grateful Processing of Unpleasant Memories," *Journal of Positive Psychology*, 3 (2008): 87–99.

13. Chad M. Burton and Laura A. King, "Effects of (Very) Brief Writing on Health: The Two-Minute Miracle," *British Journal of Health Psychology*, 13 (2008): 9–14.

14. Anjali Mishra and Robert A. Emmons, *Sex Differences in Gratitude: Effects on Psychological Well-Being, Prosocial Behavior, Materialism, and Meaning in Life.* Poster presented at the First World Congress on Positive Psychology, Philadelphia, PA, June 2009.

15. Trinity Lutheran Church, *A Tapestry of Gratitude* (Stillwater, MN: Trinity Lutheran Church, 2009), 18.

16. Silvia Knobloch-Westerwick, Yuan Gong, Holly Hagner, and Laura Kerbeykian, "Tragedy Viewers Count Their Blessings: Feeling Low on Fiction Leads to Feeling High on Life," *Communication Research*, 39 (2012).

17. "Miracle Escapes from the Killer Wall of Black Water," *The Australian* (March 15, 2011).

18. "Gratitude and a Song of Hope from Children in Japan," *Christian Science Monitor* (March 11, 2012).

19. Jacqueline N. Ventura and Pauline G. Boss, "The Family Coping Inventory Applied to Parents with New Babies," *Journal of Marriage and the Family*, 45 (1983): 867–875.

20. Laura L. Vernon, Jacqueline M. Dillon, and Amanda R. W. Steiner, "Proactive Coping, Gratitude, and Posttraumatic Stress Disorder in College Women," *Anxiety, Stress, & Coping*, 22 (2009), 117–127.

21. Robert A. Emmons and Lisa R. Krause, *Voices from the Heart: Narratives of Gratitude and Thankfulness in Persons with Neuromuscular Diseases*, unpublished manuscript, University of California, Davis, October 2000.

22. Dan P. McAdams, *The Redemptive Self: Stories Americans Live By* (New York: Oxford University Press, 2006).

23. Ibid, 20.

24. Tim P. VanDuivendyk, *The Unwanted Gift of Grief: A Ministry Approach* (New York: Haworth, 2006).

25. Melissa Muller, *A Garden of Eden in Hell: The Life of Alice Herz-Sommer* (London: Macmillan, 2008).

Chapter Seven: The Twenty-One-Day Gratitude Challenge

1. Michael E. McCullough, Robert A. Emmons, and Jo-Ann Tsang, "The Grateful Disposition: A Conceptual and Empirical Topography," *Journal of Personality and Social Psychology*, 82 (2002): 112–127.

2. David Steindl-Rast, *Gratitude as Thankfulness and as Gratefulness*, in *The Psychology of Gratitude*, ed. R. A. Emmons and M. E. McCullough (New York: Oxford University Press, 2004).

Additional Readings

Au, Wilkie, and Au, Noreen Cannon. *The Grateful Heart: Living the Christian Message* (New York: Paulist Press, 2011).

Emmons, Robert, and Hill, Joanna. *Words of Gratitude for Mind, Body and Soul* (West Conshohocken, PA: Templeton Press, 2001).

Jensen, Todd Aaron. *On Gratitude* (Avon, MA: Adams Media, 2010).

Leddy, Mary Jo. *Radical Gratitude* (Maryknoll, NY: Orbis, 2002).

Lesowitz, Nina. *Living Life as a Thank You: The Transformative Power of Daily Gratitude* (Berkeley, CA: Viva Editions, 2009).

Lyubomirsky, Sonja. *The How of Happiness: A Scientific Approach to Getting the Life You Want* (New York: The Penguin Press, 2007).

Lyubomirsky, Sonja. *The Myths of Happiness: What Should Make You Happy but Doesn't, What Shouldn't Make You Happy, but Does* (New York: The Penguin Press, 2013).

Okitembo, Louis Ngomo. *In Everything, Give Thanks: The Power of Gratitude* (Bloomington, IN: Xlibris, 2012).

Price, Catherine. *Gratitude: A Journal* (San Francisco: Chronicle Books, 2007).

Shelton, Charles. *The Gratitude Factor: Enhancing Your Life Through Grateful Living* (New York: Hidden Spring, 2010).

Steindl-Rast, David. *Gratefulness, the Heart of Prayer* (New York: Paulist Press, 1981).

About The Author

Robert A. Emmons, PhD, is professor of psychology at the University of California, Davis, where he has taught since 1988. He received his PhD degree in personality and social ecology from the University of Illinois at Urbana-Champaign, and his bachelor's degree in psychology from the University of Southern Maine. He is the author of nearly 150 original publications in peer-reviewed journals or chapters and has written or edited five books, including *The Psychology of Ultimate Concerns* (Guilford Press), *The Psychology of Gratitude* (Oxford University Press), and *Thanks! How Practicing Gratitude Can Make You Happier* (Houghton-Mifflin). A leader in the positive psychology movement, Dr. Emmons is founding editor and editor in chief of the *Journal of Positive Psychology.* He is past president of the American Psychological Association's Division 36, Psychology of Religion. His research focuses on personal goals and purpose, spirituality, the psychology of gratitude and thankfulness, and subjective well-being. Dr. Emmons has received research funding from the National Institute of Mental Health, the John Templeton Foundation, and the National Institute on Disability and Rehabilitation Research. His research has been featured in dozens of popular media outlets including the *New York Times*, *USA Today*, *U.S. News & World Report*, *Newsweek*, *Time*, NPR, PBS, *Christianity Today*, *Consumer Reports*, and *Reader's Digest*. He lives with his wife, Yvonne, and their two sons, Adam and Garrett, in Davis, California.

Index